LANDLESS IN SEATTLE

Edited by
DANIELLE HARVEY

Copyright © 2023 by Peanut Butter Publishing

ISBN: 978-1-59849-330-6

Library of Congress Control Number: 2022920156

BISAC Code:
LCO000000 LITERARY COLLECTIONS / General

Printed in Korea

Editor: Danielle Harvey
Design: Soundview Design

www.landlessinseattle.com

All rights reserved. No part of this book may be transmitted in any form or by any means, electronic or mechanical, including photocopying, recording, or by any information storage or retrieval system, in part, in any form, without the permission of the author.

Requests for such permissions should be addressed to:

Peanut Butter Publishing
Seattle, Washington 98102
206-860-4900
www.peanutbutterpublishing.com

Peanut Butter Publishing was founded fifty-one years ago on a houseboat.

Table of Contents

Acknowledgments	vii
From the Floating Homes Association President	ix
Introduction from the Editor	xi
Short Stories	1
Art	147
Poetry	179
Photography	185
Closing Thoughts	239

Acknowledgments

Peanut Butter Publishing would like to acknowledge those who made this book possible: its contributors, editor, designer, the Floating Homes Association, and the floating homes that line the docks of Seattle—inspiring all the art captured within these pages.

Thank you.

From the Floating Homes Association President

Greetings, floating-home members and friends.

Did you know that approximately sixty years ago, the City of Seattle passed new code requiring houseboats to be tied to the city sewer system? It was a good code because prior to then we were flushing directly into the lake! However, there was one big problem…the code provided absolutely no transition time for our community to make the change. In a time span of six months, we lost forty-five floating homes located south of Newton Street on Fairview. This event spurred  one of our resident activists, Terry Pettus, together with others, to form what is today's Floating Homes Association, which successfully blocked further condemnations.

Thirty years later, we lost another twelve homes to evictions by dock landlords who realized they could evict and build new homes at great profit. To mitigate that, the FHA worked tirelessly to pass what is today's Equity Ordinance, effectively providing rights and protections from random evictions by dock owners.

Today, the FHA faces a seemingly innocuous new electrical code requiring all floating homes to put their meters on shore. But we've learned, based on hard data from two docks, that the cost to comply is approximately $74,000 per houseboat, or a community expense of $24 to $28 million. We're opposing this and proposing a negotiated outcome that both improves the life-safety of our existing system while removing the electrical utility from the liability for those elements on or in our docks over which Seattle City Light has no control.

Unlike a home on land, our community is subject to the rules and regulations of the City of Seattle, the Shorelines Management Act, the Department of Natural Resources, the Army Corps of Engineers, Seattle City Light, and others to name but a few. A change in the regulations of any one of these agencies can have a great impact on us.

Our world afloat on the lake is an incredible privilege. We live in a unique environment surrounded by stunning nature and exciting wildlife in the context of true community. It doesn't get much better! But this unique and rich lifestyle is based on constant vigilance, which for our community, is your Floating Homes Association.

On behalf of the FHA Board, thank you for your past and ongoing support that allows our community to thrive.

Peter Erickson
President FHA

Introduction from the Editor

Seattle, Washington, is a place for brilliant artists, eloquent writers, and eclectic voices. Though it's a large metropolitan area, its people hold an unrivaled connection to nature and culture. One of its most unique communities is the floating homes, where all walks of life come together on the water. To live on a floating home, a sense of adventure and a healthy relationship with risk are required. It's not a lifestyle for the faint of heart or one many will experience, where the front yard is a dock, the back is a lake, and the rooftop a place to wave to your neighbors.

One of these distinctive personalities wondered: *What kind of stories do floating homes residents have to offer?* Being a houseboat owner himself, Elliott Wolf wanted to see what artistry was behind his fellow Seattleites' doors. It was no surprise that the call was answered by photographers, artists, and writers—all ready to share their pictures of existence, depictions of days spent on unstable ground, and stories of lives well-lived.

As the editor of *Landless in Seattle*, I wanted to gather pieces that anthologized a space rarely explored within the Emerald City. What I found was a group of people wanting nothing more than to share what life on the water really means. Though it's easy to romanticize the sunsets, the egrets outside your window, and sipping cocktails with your legs cooling off, there's a side seldom seen, such as invasive looky-loos, rouge litter and rising pollution, and aging homes older than their inhabitants.

Creative expression is how humans share perspective, and this collection of works invites its readers to appreciate and understand floating homes and their people—who know their pocket of paradise floats on history but is everchanging with the times.

So I invite you to read their stories and poems, admire their photos, and lose the sense of living on land through their art. Then maybe you'll look at those rows of beautiful, colorful floating homes a little differently.

Danielle Harvey
Senior Executive Editor at Peanut Butter Publishing

Short Stories

We all have stories to tell, but these are from the voices of those who have experienced life on the water. Living on a floating home has moved these writers to share their fiction, nonfiction, and poetic prose. Leave land behind as you read these pieces inspired by a day-to-day without it.

How We Floated Home
by Amalia Walton and Lilian Gregorich

AMALIA

On that very first day, May 18, 1980, the wind blew from the west. It carried a plume of ash, emitted from Mount Saint Helens, like night crossing the sky. The volcano erupted all day and into the late afternoon as my mother and I moved our small collection of mismatched belongings into our floating house, olive-green with countertops printed like space-aged boomerangs. We moved more things out that day than in, discarding the broken furniture left behind by the previous inhabitants.

A few of my mother's friends, in mustard-colored corduroy, carried our belongings. First down the stairs and then down the dock, staring up at the sky for clues about what the day would bring. My mother was young, newly divorced, and taking notice of who showed up to help. Not necessarily the people she was expecting. It was a quiet day. No one came out of their homes, and anything was possible. The grownups took turns climbing onto the roof to look at the plume of ash. Afterwards, I stood on the front deck but not too close to the edge.

In our new home, we had curtains instead of cabinet doors, a clawfoot bathtub, and a toaster oven fire every day before breakfast. A thrifted side table made of dark, unfinished wood held old copies of the *New Yorker* and Margaret, my goldfish who lived longer than anyone expected. Each morning, I woke in my crib and brushed the tips of my fingers across the rough cedar wall that shone silver in first light. Next, I stood, gripping the rail with my hands, and cried out to see if someone would arrive to comfort me. My mother appeared every time, through the slightly too small door of my bedroom, installed upside down and backwards.

The houseboat at Flo Villa was our first home together, just the two of us. That year we would turn two and thirty respectively, living snugly, as Terry Petus used to say, in God's pocket.

When summer came, the lake smelled fertile and earthy. I watched dark, wet footprints evaporate on the deck, shrinking from something recognizable to the tracks of exotic birds and then disappearing altogether. I felt the dock carpet, fuzzy and white-hot under my feet. My summer uniform was a bright-blue life jacket adorned with a patch from the local aquarium. *If you fall in*, my mother said, *you will sink to the bottom, and I won't get you back.* The edge of the deck was sharp under my chin as I lay on my belly and watched for fish. When the light hit just right, I could see all the way to the bottom.

My mother made friends with our neighbors, two doctors in training, a retired schoolteacher, and a woman who would later leave us to become a nun on a small island to the north. She left behind a cardboard box filled with colored pencils and a day planner from the year she moved away. I wondered if anyone counted days on the island. At our house, we fell into a rhythm. We baked bread, we took the bus to the aquarium to visit the octopus, and every day we paddled our boat on the lake. The skin of the boat was taught like a drum, and the seats were smooth ovals of honey-colored wood. After we cleared the interior of spiders, I lowered myself onto the rear seat and my mother handed me a peanut-butter sandwich. Wheat bread, no jelly. I held the snack in my left hand, slowly nibbling at the soft edges until the bread and filling became one under the pressure of my fingers. The other hand I hung over the side of the boat, dragging five digits across the surface of the water, transfixed by the wavy "V" shape that grew wider and wider behind us. The boat was the safest place in my world.

In the evening, my mother cooked dinner in our galley kitchen while I stood on my highchair and kept her company with my chatter. We often retired to the living room after this and watched through the big sliding-glass doors as the sun set and the lights across the lake began to sparkle. All around us were the tidy, spare homes of our neighbors, the sounds of dinner dishes being washed and dried, and the murmurs of a day coming to close.

Twenty-six years later, I would stand on the deck of that house with my newborn, listening to those same sounds as I tried to soothe her in the unusual heat of early September. It was a Tuesday evening—race night. I bounced her sweaty, diapered body in my arms and watched the sailboats cut close around the buoys.

LILIAN

The first time I set foot on a sailboat, I was two years old. The boat belonged to my grandfather and was moored to our floating home. I boarded the boat with my mother, who was clinging tightly to the handle of my bulky life jacket. Once aboard, I got to exploring. My keen eyes found the corner of the deck where all the spiders cowered from the sunlight. My little hands and growling belly discovered the wooden shelf where the Fritos and Clif Bars were stored. The ache in my tiny bladder was relieved to find the tiny toilet tucked in the V-berth. I fell in love with the boat, a world in miniature, sized just right for my small body.

A boat, however, isn't the only thing needed for sailing. You also need skill, something that must be learned. My mother and I decided that the best way to learn this skill was at a sailing camp. At the camp, we students sat on the wooden dock and learned knots, points of sail, and how to avoid collision. On the water, we did drill after drill in boats that were shaped like bathtubs and never caught any wind. My partner and I only completed half the drills, and by the end of our day on the water, we were both shedding tears of frustration. We were frustrated with each other, the instructors, the boat, but most of all with the wind. The wind saw our struggles. She watched as we tried to bully her into carrying us across the water, but she kept her distance, choosing instead to fill the sails of other boats. She became my enemy.

The next summer, I did not return to that sailing camp. The summer after that, I still did not want anything to do with a sailboat. Finally, two years later, I decided to try again. I chose a new place to sail and a new kind of boat. The hull was nearly flat, and this boat, a Laser, caught every whisper of wind. I learned every inch of it, from the silky ends peeking out of the frayed sheets, to the scratchy foam covering the hiking straps. The next summer, I returned to the Laser. I took it out of the marina and through Portage Bay, inching toward Lake Washington. The smooth water silently returned my stare, and the wind lazed somewhere far away. The boat and I drifted and drifted, nudged by wakes, and a ghost of wind. After an eternity of patience, the wind gave in and graced me with her presence. I felt her first in a tug of the rough rope against my calloused hands as she filled my sail, rounding its rainbow stripes. Then I saw her. Dancing on the tips of the waves: twirling, twisting, and jumping. I heard her whisper in my ears as I flew across the water, telling me to let her carry me faster. I tasted her on my lips as she teased me with spray. In a single gust, the wind lifted the boat and cleared my mind, her cool fingertips brushing away my worries. Alongside the wind, I was lighter than air. Even as my ankles screamed in pain from the aging hiking straps and tendrils of hair whipped my face, I felt like I was flying. I was finally free.

My first experience with a sailboat was fraught with limitations. I was tethered to the house, to a life jacket, and to my mother. As I grew older, I carried this history of physical confinement with me. The physical limitations morphed into mental tethers. Rules, limits, and fear fogged my mind, tethering me to myself. I let myself believe my own projected limitations were the essence of sailing. The whispering of the wind told me otherwise. So did the joy I felt flying across the water. The only thing a sailor should be tethered to is the wind. Now that I've embraced that, I can fly.

AMALIA

My baby girl grew up and learned to fly, with our house on the lake as her beacon and our channel as her landing strip. She also learned the comfort of boats, the way I had learned it growing up there on the lake. So that one day, when she, her little brother, and I became a family of three rather than four, we knew exactly what to do.

I was young and newly divorced. We took stock of our belongings, moving some things in and some things out. We noted who was there to carry the heavy things and reach the tall shelves those first weeks and months. The world didn't stop this time, because we were the only ones who heard the explosion.

The floating house was reborn yet again. We tore out the ceilings and the floors. We peered through the holes into the lake and shivered at the thought of what might come up. I painted gold patches in the living room, like islands, and we had dance parties with the lights out. I got rid of the television and wired custom brass fixtures from New Orleans all by myself. A brave undertaking after the infamous thermostat-replacement fire. It was mostly smoke. We added a loft bedroom so we could retreat to our own corners, but no one ever did. The neighbors were equal parts helpful, indignant, and angry for us, depending on what was needed in the moment. They had been our family all along.

Nights were the hardest, but history told us to get in the boat where it was safe. On a late-night visit to Home Depot, we discovered blinking red arm bands, and we wore them with our life jackets as we slid silently off the edge of the deck and into the boat like pirates. We sat in the same order every night—daughter, son, mother—as we paddled down the channel past our neighbors washing dinner dishes. After a brief pause at the last house to look both ways, we glided out onto the lake. Here was another world: quiet, dark, and still. We were alone together in our floating cocoon, protected between the two hills. Anything was possible.

Our kayaking ritual lasted deep into the winter. In December, I found the sparklers that were left from my wedding. The children asked if they were still safe. "Yes," I told them, because I needed them to be. Because I couldn't throw them away and I couldn't keep them in the house. In the light of the kitchen, I explained to the children how sparklers worked, which end to hold and to drop them in the water if it was hot or they felt scared. I promised it was okay, just this once, to drop something in the lake that didn't belong there. We put on our life jackets and our blinking arm bands and paddled to the very middle, like skimming over a sheet of glass. We sat still until the boat stopped rocking and all we heard were the muffled sounds of engines revving and slowing on Interstate 5. Far away there was a siren, and even farther, the loud pop of a car backfiring. The last drips fell from the curved edges of our paddles, making ever-expanding rings on the surface of the lake. When the rings had smoothed, I carefully lit the rough ends of the sparklers. In succession, from bow to stern, our sputtering lights joined with the glittering, saw-toothed skyline. We wrote our names above the water because the lake was ours.

LON-MARIE

Forty years after Mount Saint Helens erupted, I turned seventy. I've never cared much about my birthday. I prefer the backstage role of celebrating others rather than myself. But as I contemplated my seven decades, I thought of my grandchildren and their mother, and I knew there was one place to thank for the people I love most in this world. The lake gave me and my daughter the new beginning we needed. It birthed the person I am today, and it was where I belonged on such a momentous birthday.

The day before, my daughter had lost a deck chair to an unexpected windstorm, and she needed my help retrieving it. We assembled the rescued buoys that hang on the side of the house, large hooks from my grandson's early attempts at fishing, and moldering lines from a pile near the grill, hoping the combination of lost things would be enough to find our whole. Our hooks got caught on items we didn't care to resurrect: an ancient plastic deck chair, an old tomato cage. There was no sign of my second husband's favorite hammer, the neighbor's wedding band, or my granddaughter's hand-painted teacup. They were lost forever in the muck. The things we keep at the bottom of the lake are both here and not here. It is a storage locker of memories.

When the dark form at the end of my line revealed itself as my daughter's chair, I called out in excitement. My family came running through the big glass doors from the living room, calling back in celebration. After the chair was safely secured on the deck, I took a step back and looked at the house. I remembered the irises that had once bloomed through a hole in the deck and two generations of fences, now removed, that kept the little ones safely out of the water. My eyes traveled to the high ceilings and wide beams of my daughter's remodel, more open and generous than the house of forty years ago. Then I took a step forward, into the arms of my thankful family, and I realized that the house had grown because we had. As our lives expanded, so did our home on the lake, and it was still holding us.

Mi Sueno

by Heidi Dellafera Eagleton

We were heading to the Ballard Locks and almost at the Fremont Bridge when, looking toward Lake Union, I yelled, "Stop, pull over. Look at that!" I was with my best friend since graduate school. He pulled into a parking space. I jumped out of his Honda coupe and bolted towards the lake. We were business partners in architecture and I, from Houston, was visiting him in Seattle, where he had set up our satellite office. It was my first trip there. He followed closely behind shouting, "For God's sake, Heidi, watch the traffic." But I barely heard him.

I sprinted down steep steps and stopped at the entrance to a dock lined with small colorful houses floating on the water. They were flush with flowers of all varieties and hues. Ferns grew out from their supporting log foundations. Kayaks and sailboats moored in waterways off narrow, street-like canals bobbed and weaved with the lake's gentle current. Each house had its own personality and character.

That was eight years after *Sleepless in Seattle*. I loved the movie, not so much for the love story, but for the floating home on the water. Now there I was, eight years later, staring at my star of the movie, the *Sleepless in Seattle* floating home at the end of a dock alongside similarly situated houses. I never thought that one day I would stand in front of it: a two-story, light-gray, shingled house with a long, windowed porch, scalloped canopy, and a wraparound deck opening to Lake Union. A chair sat on a four-foot by six-foot boat dock off the main deck, unoccupied. I fell in love. I had no idea where fate was taking me that day, but I would find out it was leading me to a place where I never imagined I would go.

"Hey, how wonderful was that, seeing the *Sleepless in Seattle* floating home up close and personal," I said that evening over a "famous clam chowder" dinner at a Seattle landmark, a local seafood restaurant on Lake Union.

"Yeah, sure, it was wonderful, but how's your chowder?" my friend questioned. "Does it have lots of clams in it?"

"Clams? Ah, I guess, but I never expected to see it. It's so much better in person. The lake is spectacular. Don't you think? And the house was just sitting there at the end of the dock with a view toward downtown. Clams, yes, ah, lots of clams. WOW, I'll never forget it."

"Would you like some more wine?" he asked. "I'll pour."

"And the fact that Tom Hanks' character in the movie, Sam Baldwin, was an architect just like us. Well now, how much better could it get? By the way, did you say something about wine?"

He stopped talking. Giving up, he sat back in his chair, folded his arms, sighed, and listened to me carrying on.

We said our goodbyes at SeaTac shortly after our trip to Ballard. The Pacific Northwest had made a big and lasting impression on me and reminded me in many ways of New England, where I was born and raised. Both celebrated the outdoors and the natural order of things. I was particularly obsessed with a "pocket neighborhood" in Langley on Whidbey Island, which we had visited earlier in the week. It was called "a neighborhood within a neighborhood." The neighborhood provided an opportunity for privacy and customized, individualized homes with a strong sense of community. It was "a place where diversity was a major asset, and where each neighbor brought their interest, energy, and passions to the effort to create a better, more vibrant living environment leading to neighbors that enjoy and care about each other." The neighborhood moved me as much as the *Sleepless in Seattle* floating home had done. I vowed on the plane back to Houston that I would build a "pocket neighborhood" there.

It wouldn't be easy. The "pocket neighborhood" I had seen was in Langley, a small waterfront village on an island in Puget Sound, a short ferry ride from Mukilteo. Houston was a large sprawling city in the Southwest marked with spaghetti-like highways, tall buildings, big houses, big cars, big trucks, and gargantuan hamburgers smothered with bacon and Jack cheese. Langley and Houston couldn't be more different.

Nonetheless, I knew my "pocket neighborhood" would be just like the one in Langley. Characteristically, it would have no less than five and no more than fifteen houses facing a commons area. Parking would be off site to encourage walking and interaction among neighbors. The houses would be small and efficient with no unnecessary spaces. They all would have front porches. And my "pocket neighborhood" would be about a lifestyle, like the Langley neighborhood, not like more conventional Houston living styles where no one knows your name. The truth was it would be an anomaly and a difficult sell.

It took a certain amount of hutzpah to even consider it. Getting people to park in something other than an attached two- or three-car garage and walk to their houses through a commons area was more than most Houstonians could fathom, particularly in the rain. But I was determined, optimistic, and a little bit stubborn. After all, "If I built it, they will come!"

My optimism quickly turned to frustration in 2017 when I had the opportunity to develop and build my "pocket neighborhood." It was then when I learned, after researching the "hows" of making it happen, that the mountain I had to climb in Houston was steep and that its peak was hidden way beyond the clouds.

Langley's "pocket neighborhood" was handed to its residents tied up in a neat little bow. There, the city, with the help of the developer and architect, promoted its living style by enacting building codes that line by line included "pocket neighborhood" characteristics. Banks were bypassed. The project was funded by its developer and architect, their families, and their friends. But it was the Pacific Northwest, after all, home to new and enlightened ideas. The stage was set, and the production was to become an instant hit.

On the other hand, in Houston, the political winds and the banking industry were less than enthusiastic. Big developer-driven building codes favored larger, car-dominant neighborhoods, the antithesis of "pocket neighborhoods." Every code page presented another hurdle. The most troublesome, neighborhood streets had to be wide, twenty-eight feet to be exact, with turnarounds every two hundred feet for firetrucks. That alone could destroy any sense of community. Private funding, unlike in Langley, was not an option. Funding was directed to big projects with big returns. And risk-adverse loan officers weren't interested in sticking their necks out for a concept that wasn't Texas "friendly."

Still, I persevered. I bought a neglected two-acre plot for my "pocket neighborhood" in an old, semi-rural African American community ten miles from downtown Houston. Through creative design and a willingness to allocate almost an acre of my property to a commons area by sacrificing profit margin, I was able to create a sense of community and still comply with Houston's building codes. To finance its construction, I agreed to build affordable houses in the area to become eligible for community development funding.

Ultimately, after many difficult and stressful months, my dream evaporated right before my eyes. The city showed no mercy, the banks even less. After building four affordable houses, the city pulled the plug on the affordable housing program my company was a part of. Banks ran for the hills. With no affordable housing, there would be no bank financing. With no financing, there would be no "pocket neighborhood." I would sell my derelict property to a big city developer who could afford to sit it out until land prices got more valuable to build a big city developer neighborhood. It was Houston, Texas, after all, home to the big everything.

I was heartbroken. I had failed.

In July, I took a much-needed break from Houston with my husband, Kevin. He was quiet on the drive from Mukilteo to Seattle except for an occasional grumble about my plan to spend the last weekend of our Pacific Northwest vacation in the city. We had just visited our younger son and his family, who had moved to Mukilteo from Houston a few years back. Kevin didn't do much to hide his feelings. He was convinced that Seattle would be the low point of our trip. My goal was to get him to agree to my six-month plan, six months in Seattle near our Mukilteo family and six months in Houston near our older son and his family. So, I let him grumble, saying nothing.

Once in Seattle, I was again en route to the Ballard Locks by way of the Fremont Bridge. I had rented a snazzy little black, vintage-looking Volkswagen convertible. The top was down. Kevin was in the passenger seat. I pointed to the floating homes on the way and said, "Look, aren't they great?" Kevin shrugged his shoulders and stared straight ahead. *Oh, that went well*, I thought to myself.

To make things more interesting for our weekend and to satisfy an item on my bucket list, I rented a 200-square-foot houseboat on a Westlake marina. Kevin, who had to live with me while my "pocket neighborhood" heartache was healing, had agreed to stay on it. To be honest, he was as thrilled with staying on a houseboat as he was with being in Seattle. Before we even got there, he was convinced that our "houseboat adventure" would be a disaster.

As luck would have it, Seattle friends, a couple we had known for years, were house sitting for a floating home on Fairview Avenue that weekend and had invited us to join them for dinner on its deck. Over a glass of wine and prosciutto-wrapped asparagus, they told us that many floating home aficionados thought this one with its orange tile roof and blue walls was as good as it got. It faced downtown Seattle, a clear shot from its deck, which that night was a glow of colors. Long skinny, green, blue, and yellow shadows from building lights reflected across the lake. The shaft of the Space Needle was a brilliant red, its observation deck lights bright white like a beacon calling sailors back to port. We sat on the deck under the stars, eating a brilliantly prepared fresh salmon dinner, staring at the skyline. It knocked Kevin's socks off.

Things were instantly brighter back at our Westlake houseboat for the remainder of the weekend. We were twenty-somethings again. It was so narrow that we had to crawl over each other and our suitcases to get into a pull-out sofa bed at night. To get into the refrigerator, we had to close the door to the deck, and the shower was barely big enough for one. The entry lock to the marina gate was always trouble. But, even with its quirks, we had coffee on its deck every morning and tandem kayaked around Lake Union every afternoon. It was beyond relaxing and peaceful. My heart was beating more steadily now.

Sharing a bottle of Cabernet on the deck of our houseboat rental, we discussed the weekend as it was coming to an end.

"Well, what do you think?" I asked Kevin, taking a big gulp of wine. "Was staying on a houseboat all that bad?"

"Hmm, other than when you jabbed me in the ribs with your

elbow rolling over in bed the other night and having to wait until you got out of the shower to use the bathroom this morning, I'd say it was good, tight, but not bad for a weekend. The deck and kayaking were great, though," he added, smiling broadly.

"Do you think owning a floating home in Seattle is in our future, maybe after we retire?" I wondered aloud. "You seem to have done a one-eighty since we've been in Seattle staying on the houseboat."

"I'm still not one hundred percent sure about buying a home on the water," he answered. "Let's rent one for a month next summer. A dry run. Would that work for you?" he asked.

"Are you kidding?" I said, clinking his glass.

The following summer in 2018, we rented a quaint little red floating home on a dock on the east side of Lake Union for the month of August. Unlike our Westlake houseboat, this rental had 1,100 square feet and a roof deck.

Although we share lots of common interests, when it comes to decision making, Kevin and I are like day and night, kind of like the Pacific Northwest and the Southwest. Kevin is a cup half empty kind of guy. He's deliberate and thoughtful. He doesn't jump in the pond before testing the water. Me, I'm a cup run-it-over kind of girl. I'm impulsive and quick and jump in without giving it much thought. Sometimes I find out the hard way that the water is freezing.

But this time would be different. We would strangely end up somewhere in the middle. For not long after we arrived on our Eastlake floating home rental, we found our balance. I was his yin, and he was my yang, and he was about to give me the surprise of a lifetime over dinner one evening in mid-August at an Italian restaurant on Eastlake, which would become a favorite.

"Hey, Heidi, let's buy a floating home on Fairview," he causally said.

"What? We've only been here a couple of weeks, and now you're telling me that you want to buy a floating home? What's up? Not that I'm complaining, but why the drastic change? It's so out of character."

"Well," he began, "I love walks around Lake Union. I love kayaking every day and not having to drive to restaurants. I love drinking wine on the upper deck with friends, watching the sunset over the Fremont Bridge. I loved the hiking excursion we took in the Cascades last week with our family. I love the Eastlake floating homes community. And I love Pete's sandwiches."

"WOW, that's amazing," I said.

"To be honest, I've been thinking about it for a long time," he said with a wink. "So, we agree?"

"Oh yeah." Without hesitation, I jumped in with both feet.

The next day, I set the wheels in motion. I met a Goldendoodle on Fairview. At the end of his leash was a real estate agent, who had been in the sale and purchase of floating homes for years. Matter of fact, he lived in one just down the street from our rental. After hugs and cuddles with his Doodle, I asked him to be our scout. He emailed floating home listings to me on a regular basis after that.

One floating home, on a dock off Fairview, caught my eye in October. Our agent previewed it. Our friends went by as well. A phone call later from the three of them, and I booked a weekend flight to Seattle. I would meet them there. I landed midday the following Saturday, grabbed a rental car, and made a beeline to Lake Union and the floating home I was scheduled to see. Our Mukilteo family met me there too.

I stood at the entry and stared down the dock. There it was, my "pocket neighborhood." Just like the one in Langley, it was a "neighborhood within a neighborhood." It had fifteen houses facing a commons area, a six-foot-wide dock running down the middle of them. Parking was off site. The houses were small and unique, no two were painted alike. Flowers, small trees in pots, and native plants graced each porched entry.

It felt like a place with a strong sense of community and "a place where diversity was a major asset." It felt like "a place where each owner brought their interest, energy, and passion to create a vibrant living environment." It felt like "a place where neighbors enjoyed and cared about each other." It felt like how my "pocket neighborhood" in Houston was supposed to feel.

I fell in love again. I skipped down the dock; it was a small light-blue house sitting on giant logs floating on the water. It had white trim and slanted exterior walls reminding me of a New England lighthouse. Its three west-facing exterior decks looked outward toward Lake Union and Queen Anne Hill. And best of all, at night, downtown Seattle and the Space Needle awash with colored lights could be seen from its upper decks and through a large master bedroom window.

At the end of the weekend, I returned to Houston with a sales contract in hand.

"It's a funny thing about dreams," I said to Kevin, who picked me up at the airport. "They don't always turn out the way you imagine. Sometimes they don't turn out at all. Yet sometimes they turn out but not exactly the way you thought they would. Sometimes, if you're lucky, when you least expect it, they take a direction beyond your wildest fantasies." Kevin looked at me and smiled.

I was lucky. I wouldn't build my dream; I would live it. I would live in a "pocket neighborhood," and one that curiously was on the water. Just before Christmas, we closed on our floating home.

And I called it "Mi Sueno."

Astrophysics, Grief, and Houseboats
An Astrophysicist Finds a New Home for a New Life
by Toby Burnett

Five years ago, in early December, I had just become the owner of a Seattle floating home! A major step forward in my new life. With my new keys, alone inside the bare place, I decided where to put my desk. I picked a corner of an upstairs room where the previous owner used to watch TV. There I had a view down the rest of the dock, unfortunately blocked at the end by another houseboat, but at least a bit of Queen Anne hill on the other side of Lake Union was visible above it. I like being able to look up from my screen and into the distance. I'd brought a small folding table and chair to try it out. It would be a month before I would sell my Fremont condo, move, and set up my desk at this spot.

Why was this my first decision regarding how I would use the place? I had recently retired as a UW physics professor but was still doing research with data from the NASA mission, *Fermi*, which I had had a lot to do with designing, getting approved, built, and launched in 2008. This had been an important part of my identity for twenty-five years, seldom far from my thoughts. For that, all I needed was a computer connected to the internet. But spending a good fraction of the day pursuing this passion also required a comfortable setting: a home office.

About that passion. From early childhood I loved to try to

understand how things worked. I was fascinated early on by the planetary system, the phases of the moon and seasons. That fascination led me to study physics and become a particle physicist. Back then, we knew very little; in the time since there has been a remarkable explosion in understanding how the Universe works at a fundamental level—an exciting time in which I got to participate. When I was starting, my original interest, astronomy, was rather boring, with no hint of the explosion to come. Then, the only way to observe the universe was optical telescopes. Pulsars, quasars, and black holes, which I study now, were unknown, as were the still-mysterious dark matter and dark energy. The two fields now overlap, so most astronomers are astrophysicists—my current field. So, I now observe the universe with the most powerful version of light, gamma rays. Despite, and because of, all these revelations, there are new mysteries and questions that continue to excite people like me. Like those "dark" things and the ultimate fate of the Universe.

Why was this a "new life"? While sitting there, I reflected on the tumultuous twenty months that led up to that moment, partly by reviewing the journal I had kept.

The first hint at what was to come was on Super Bowl Sunday, notable for the Seahawks' triumph. Before the game, however, Joan, my wife and best friend for forty years, fainted in the bathroom. I found her in a pool of blood from a head wound. That was not itself serious, but the event represented a figurative sword hanging over us. What did it mean? What was going to happen next?

The answer came three weeks later. I was at a meeting with my NASA collaborators at Stanford, just waking up in my hotel room on the last day. Checking my email, I found a note from Joan's son that she was in the hospital with a collapsed central lobe of her right lung. I rushed home to find that she was having an MRI scan, which would detect a second tumor in her brain, implying that she had lung cancer which had metastasized, and therefore was stage IV. Median survival is two years, I was soon to learn.

That night, alone in our condo, was the first time I cried, as it started to sink in that my future life had been shattered. I was semi-retired but still teaching and supervising a final graduate student, so I was looking forward to extensive travel with Joan while pursuing my research.

The next two months, all we had left, were a nightmare, terminated by an opportunistic pneumonia. Up to then, I had been in a daze, reacting to the situation, supporting Joan as best I could. Now I was truly on my own. I had earlier set up Caring Bridge as a mechanism to share her status with friends and family, and to coordinate offers of help. My last entry:

> On April 22, at 2:30 PM, with me, her son, all three stepchildren, and daughter-in-law around the bed, we had the respirator tube removed. I held her hand as she took her last, ineffective breaths. This was in accordance with her health directive. After consultation with the internist and oncologist, we decided that the possibility of a cure was so remote, and quality of life (now intubated) so bad, that we would let her go.
> I have very much appreciated this forum to allow friends and family to understand what was happening.
> Now I'm the one in great need.
> She came into this world on valentine's day, lived a loving life, and returned to earth on Earth day, 72 years later.

Indeed, I had no idea what I was getting into.

Much has been written about grief, especially in the last several years, but two quotes now stick out in my mind; from Shakespeare, "Everyone can master a grief but he that has it," and from a recent memoir by Long Litt Woon, *The Way Through the Woods*, "Grief grinds slowly; it devours all the time it needs."

I had a lot of help initially from my family, especially my daughter, who took me under her wing and took me to stay with her family for the first few weeks. But for people in my state, the Shakespeare quote resonates in that there are so few people who seem to understand. Grief support groups are invaluable for that, as I was to find. I was spared the physical symptoms that many experience. But I was unable to muster the concentration required to pursue my research. I was fortunate to have a very capable T.A. to run the physics lab that I taught that autumn.

Expanding on the second quote, it took months of searching for resources to understand what I was experiencing, what I could expect, how long it would take. A breakthrough of sorts came when I searched online for "grief turning point," in the naïve hope that there would be an epiphany, an abrupt transition to "acceptance." That connected me to Pat Bertram's blog, and to her book *Grief: The Great Yearning*. It was an invaluable description of her first year full of her experiences and discoveries about the process. That included debunking the "five stages of grief" as inappropriate. The answer to the question turned out to be that one may expect things to start improving after eighteen months—hardly the turning point I had hoped for. The book was organized as an entry for each of many days, labeled with the day number. A second resource was *Healing After Loss: Daily Meditations For Working Through Grief* by Martha Whitmore Hickman. My morning routine was to read the entry for that date from *Healing After Loss*, and the entry, if there was one, from Bertram's book for my corresponding day. Then, or whenever I felt the need, I expressed my thoughts in my journal.

An unexpected manifestation of my profound grief was a strong empathetic reaction to some deaths, resonating with my own grieving state. Two incidents stand out: the death of Robin

Williams and the death of forty-two people in the Oso landslide north of Seattle. I had always admired Robin Williams, and the fact that he took his life the same way as my father, a life-changing event when I was fifteen, especially got to me. The Oso landslide happened during my horrible two months; I was only dimly aware of it at the time. Then, many months later at the roadside memorial, I could not look at the devastated landscape without breaking down. As I wrote at the time, "As I absorbed the facts I found that just looking at that jumbled landscape where forty-two people died on that day, I was overwhelmed with grief—empathy and association with my own loss. Just writing this now brings it back in powerful waves."

From my journal at the anniversary of Joan's death:

> The day is here. The clock ticked over while I was lying awake at midnight.
>
> I read the April 22 meditation in Healing After Loss, completing the cycle.
>
> And I've now read to the end of Pat's book. I'm now also a 1-year grief survivor. She has been a great companion in my grief, expressing my sorrow so eloquently.
>
> I did not expect to react like this, crying as the day starts. I am clearly a lot better than earlier in this process, but I'll never really "get over" the loss of my dear soul mate. We did not communicate so much verbally, but we each knew how important the other was. I was always so proud to be with her. In public gatherings, I felt so content to have her as such an intimate partner, often aware of the admiration of others at our bond. The bond that no longer exists, at least in this plane of existence. Are you there, somewhere, Joan? Of course in my thoughts and memories.

In the summer, I started seriously looking for a houseboat to buy.

For twenty-three years, Joan and I had lived in a Fremont condo with a sweeping view to the south and east, dominated by Mt. Rainer when it was "out," and including Lake Union with a direct line of sight to what would be my new home. But it was no longer "home." I knew that I needed to move, part of establishing a new identity. I referred to my "new life" many times in my journal, as I struggled to define it. I had never lived alone before.

An important goal for the new life that I was seeking was to join a community, which was lacking in the condo. I toyed with joining a senior community for a while. But by that first summer, my focus turned to finding a houseboat. This is an option unique to Seattle, and quite a dramatic break. I wanted to stay close to the UW as well—one of the members of my UW Physics department had had one and famously commuted by kayak. My resolve was enforced thanks to a friend who lived in Eastlake, only a few blocks from where I wound up. She took me to a party with her walking group to a modest houseboat on the end of a dock just down the street. I had a long discussion with the owner about how they so loved it and had raised children there.

One thing that the search made clear was how varied the older houseboats are. The one I bought, now five years ago, the third that I looked at, came onto the market at exactly the right time. It fit in with its red exterior and interesting structural details. Buying a floating home has some additional hurdles compared with general real estate; one needs to have an inspection beneath it, to check the additional floatation, the log raft itself being insufficient, and options for financing and insurance are limited. But all that came together, leading to that moment.

A separate thread in my struggle to define a new life and identity was a search for a compatible companion. That long and at times arduous story came to a very satisfying conclusion with Wanda's finding  me. She then gave me valuable help and advice during the houseboat search. At that time, we were dating—now we are partners.

The hope for a compatible, supportive community has been richly met. One aspect that I now appreciate is the variety of ages of my neighbors, from young professionals to the older cohort, some having lived here several decades.

I genuinely enjoy this comfortable environment.

I finish with two journal entries at the end of that year:

> So, 2015 about to end. Ending is a lot more upbeat than the end of 2014, the worst year of my life. 2016 will be the second full year without Joan. My life certainly has taken abrupt turns. At times like now, I consider with amazement how unexpected, and satisfying, my current situation is.

Last day of this transition year. Transition from overpowering grief to optimistically planning a future. From the condo to the houseboat. And to Wanda.

My Bromance with Bernie
by Spider Kedelsky

When I first met him in April of 2020, he was a mess. His neck and head covered in bite marks and sores, body all ruffled, walking with a decided limp. He was pitiful looking, a loner fallen on hard times, seemingly rejected by his community. Out of compassion, and restless from the first weeks of the COVID-19 lockdown, Joan and I agreed that he needed our attention.

Bernie snacking. He's started growing back his mating plumage.

With a list to starboard as he walked, Joan dubbed him Bernie the Lame Duck, after the candidate who had just ended his second run for the Democratic presidential nomination. I bridled at the suggestion since his namesake, Bernie Sanders, who had been the captain of my Brooklyn high school track team, was anything but lame. I soon thought better of it, and Bernie he became.

When first encountered, Bernie, a male mallard duck, a common sight on the waters in front of our floating home on Seattle's Portage Bay, was attired in his colorful if disheveled mating regalia. A raggedy fowl for sure, one I presumed not a babe magnet. In the months to come, that proved not to be the case.

Joan, as is her wont, immediately went online to research what a wayward duck should eat, knowing that bread is not a good option, as it can harm waterfowl. She discovered that Bernie would

In the few months when we go swimming in our cold-weather wetsuits, Bernie, sometimes joined by Big Boy, will swim almost protectively around us, coming back on the deck when we do for a well-deserved snack.

Bernie and Mini have a cross species encounter

Friendly mallards are not the only creatures with whom we share the water. While swimming during the summer, I went to the bulkhead (land) side of my floating home and noticed movement out of the corner of my eye. Turning around to face the old-growth logs beneath our home, I saw a little furry face peering at me. I peered back. Together we peered for a moment or two. A baby otter.

For several months a muskrat lived under the floating home to our west. We would see her every day diligently going out into deeper water, dragging back succulent greenery on which to feast. A few months ago, she disappeared.

Recently, while swimming in our now-cold waters, I saw a small, dark animal under the dock of that float to our west. Every now and then, a little face would pop up to eye at me. It sure looked like a mink, but a mink? Here? Later, looking at photos, that's exactly who it was. I had never seen one in our waters. Did this little animal, described as "semi-aquatic," identify me as a human or just this mysterious "other" in the water?

Which makes me wonder. Do "our" ducks recognize us? I presumed Bernie, Tiffany, and Big Boy knew us from multiple visits to our home. But what if we are somewhere else?

This past summer, Joan was swimming about 100 yards away from our float and encountered several ducks sitting on a long dock. She called out, "Bernie, is that you?" One duck got up, waddled to the end of the dock, jumped off, and swam toward Joan. He was followed by a female. It was Bernie and Tiffany. Proof of duck recognition? I leave it up to animal behaviorists to settle this.

During the summer and early fall, a large group of mallards often congregate on our waters. As seen from afar, I couldn't tell if any of them were our friends. One fail-safe strategy let me know who our people were. I keep the duck nut-and-grain mix in a small plastic box. I walk outside and rattle it loudly. If it is any of our trio, even if they are headed away from our house, they will instantly do a one-eighty and paddle full speed ahead towards me. Pavlov's ducks.

Bernie (left), Tiffany, and Big Boy
December 2020

As fall came to Seattle, the days shorter, the nights colder, I was unsure if Bernie and his cohorts would fly away to parts south or if they would stay the winter. From what I read, many do migrate, and some hang around. During winters we see a variety of ducks, though few mallards. The latter are usually the only ones we see in the warm months.

Of course, with climate change fully upon us, who knows what birds will be where and when, and who among them will fade into history, made extinct by the actions of Homo sapiens, the earth's most damaging and dangerous species.

It's mid-December, and we haven't seen Bernie for a few days. Will he be back? I don't know. Whatever may transpire next in the duck world, I do know we have enjoyed the company of these wild and agreeable creatures in the time of COVID-19.

Postscript: It's November, 2021, and Bernie returned two weeks ago and has daily feedings at Chez Kedelsky. He looks wonderful, though still limps, some days more than others. He has been joined by this year's girlfriend, Simone, who has beautiful plumage. A handsome couple with whom to share life on the water.

Lifeboats
by Debra Boyer

Neighbors whispered they were hippies. No one was sure who owned or lived in the old houseboat. Was it Nick, George, Guy, Debby, Susan, Ed, Lynne—all of them? A different mix of characters always coming and going. Neighbors were awakened by skinny dippers and swimmers laughing a little too hard. A phone call might be answered from either of two locations; rewiring enabled a few houses to use the same phone line because no one had any money. A houseboat, the perfect setting for vagabonds in 1974.

Aerial view around 1975 of 2235 Fairview Ave E, looking south

The stories of how any of them ended up on the houseboat were mired in anecdotes of sibling relocations, job losses, graduate school, divorces, social activism, broken relationships, and reconnections. As each character was trying to connect their dots, a bill of sale was signed for all of thirteen thousand dollars. George, a recent graduate of Boston University Law School and headed for legal services, found Debby, who was training his Vista lawyer group in Seattle. The old houseboat's ownership was transferred, and forty-seven years of houseboat living was launched.

Launched, repaired, and relaunched. A flotilla, an armada tied to cleats, fence posts, rafts, and to each other, ringing the houseboat, knocking in the wind. There were two motorboats, three kayaks, one wherry, a canoe, two paddleboards, a windsurfing board, and two more boats that were now home to crayfish and perch.

Each craft had a story to tell about the personalities that kept arriving.

Our first boat, our first boat story.

Reading the *Little Nickle Classifieds* (remember those?) on a Sunday morning early in our houseboat tenure, we came across an ad for a handmade wooden canoe for sale on Bainbridge Island. "Wooden" should have served as a warning in that ad. We headed out and arrived at the meeting place on the sand spit. A young woman had built the canoe and recited her adventures paddling the Salish Sea. We loaded the red and white wooden craft on top of our neighbor's VW van (what else?), headed back to the houseboat, and launched it on Lake Union.

This first boat story begins long before in my Eastern Oregon hometown, where no one had a boat. My great grandparents immigrated from Blairgowrie, Scotland, along with many other Scots, including the families of Linus Pauling, one of the twenty greatest scientists of all time. He was awarded the Nobel Prize in physiology/medicine in 1954 and the Nobel Peace Prize in 1962 for his peace activism. Linus Pauling was also well known for his clinical trials on the use of Vitamin C to prevent and alleviate the common cold.[1]

---

[1] My hometown of Condon, Oregon, boasts two Nobel Prize winners. William P. Murphy graduated from Condon High School in 1910 and in 1934 shared the Nobel Prize for physiology/medicine, specifically for development of treatment for pernicious anemia. Linus Pauling's mother died from this disease in 1926.

Dr. Pauling gave a lecture in Seattle shortly after we bought our homemade wooden canoe. We were able to speak with him after the lecture, and he remembered my family and asked about several relatives.

Pauling's Drug Store in Condon, Oregon (1905)

He was occasionally seen taking a drive through my hometown out to the ghost town of Lonerock, the location of his family homestead. A few days after the lecture, I received a call from his nephew, who was visiting Seattle. Dr. Pauling had asked him to call me; he was curious about houseboats and wanted to go for a paddle!

We paddled to Gasworks Park and pulled the canoe across the beach onto the shore. Conversation was easy with our common Oregon roots. We talked about our families' histories and the scientific achievements of Linus Pauling for a couple of hours on a surprisingly hot Seattle summer day. When it was time to return, we pushed the canoe off the beach and back in the water. We slipped in and started paddling.

Paddling, but paddling nowhere; we were going down. The boat was filling with water. I was sinking with Linus Pauling's nephew! We cut a sharp turn and headed back to Gasworks.

Looking at the bottom of the boat, we could see several rocks had gone through the hull; it looked like Swiss cheese. What to do—I was feeling a little sheepish. At first, we thought we could walk back, but both of us were barefoot. SPD Harbor Patrol was a short distance west of Gasworks Park. We walked over to the Harbor Patrol office and gently woke up the two officers on duty; it was Seattle in 1975. The good officers gave us a ride back to the houseboat in the police boat with the canoe in tow.

Dr. Pauling's nephew took his Lake Union paddling adventure with humor, and I safely drove him back to his family. I never heard from the Darling (mother's family name) or Pauling family again, but the story must have been told, at least once.

We were without a canoe for a while. But if you walk around our house and look in the slip between houseboats, you will see a faded blue (fiberglass!) canoe. Around 1984, our neighbor Andy and I decided to buy another used canoe for our spouses. The name is a not-so-clever blend of our spouses' names, Barb and George—Bargeo was something Andy and I came up with.

The canoe is one of our reminders of Andy, who left us far too soon, and of his role in the founding of DOX Cooperative in 1982. Our cooperative was the second to form on the lake. Flo Villa had incorporated some twenty years earlier when the docks were rebuilt and sewer systems installed. The DOX movement was instigated by Andy and his wife, Barb, when the Dock Lord refused to let them remodel. Andy and I also planted the wisteria gracing the trellis at the head of the dock; the plant is now thirty-five-plus years old. And the best memory: Andy married George and me in 1984.

I could not even guess how many cousins and friends have used the canoe. We have had a lot of fun with new canoers, telling them to get in the canoe, face each other, and start paddling. We paddled the DOX kids, Lily, now the university professor; David, now the artist; and Thea, now a nurse, until they could no longer fit.

Behind the Bargeo canoe is a distinctive boat known as a California Wherry. A wherry is a rowboat with a sliding seat; wherries were used in canals in England to carry cargo. It is wider and more stable than a rowing shell. And it is fast; a rower can cross the lake in a few minutes, getting a great aerobic workout.

How does a California Wherry end up at a houseboat in Seattle? The answer starts with my decision to go to graduate school and get a PhD in Anthropology, which I did in 1986. That is how we met Tom. Tom had a dilettante's interest in anthropology. His father, who owned most of the parking lots in Los Angeles (the equivalent of Joe Diamond in Seattle), thought grad school might give his son "focus." He and his wife, who left a job as the actor Nick Nolte's assistant, moved to Seattle with the wherry in tow. Tom was the life of the classroom and the life of the party, his cleverness always on display. But the goal of graduate school was too elusive, and after one gloomy winter in Seattle, sunny L.A. drew them back.

There was his wherry, still on the trailer in the driveway. "Yes, we will take it," my husband said. The wherry kept us connected to Tom and his merry and extemporaneous approach to life.

The Games of the XXIII Olympiad were hosted in Los Angeles the summer of 1984. Tom's father had the contract to clean several venues, including the LA Memorial Coliseum. At Tom's "invitation," my husband was "hired" as a sanitation worker, donned janitor clothing, and given a badge; he had free range for the track events at the games. O.J. Simpson carried the Olympic torch that year, and George had on-the-field views of Carl Lewis, Alonzo Babers, Al Joyner, Evelyn Ashford, Joan Benoit, and so many "also rans."

Wedged between Bargeo and the wherry is a weathered windsurfing board. But this is not just any windsurfing board. It is the board style designed in Europe and used by athletes in the 1984 summer Olympics, the first year windsurfing was included as a sailing event in the Olympics. It is longer and tippier than later versions and designed for speed.

How did this novel board, now transformed into a paddleboard, come to live out its last years by Bargeo?

Sometimes it takes effort to recall the connections that led to a decades' old friendship. My husband's sister's friend opened her house to multiple sojourners over the years. One was Karen, who married Matt, but no one can remember how Matt appeared.

Matt's imagination, always open to a gamble, was captured by the promise of riches to the north in Canada. A wheelin' dealin' rich adventure. In the early 1970s, Whistler, B.C., was opened to development. Matt was there. Our first visit to Whistler in the late 1970s needed a lot of imagination to match Matt's vision. Whistler was still wilderness and full of "developers" who must have been reincarnated gold rushers. Matt was all in, including obtaining a windsurfer to test out on the vastly underdeveloped five lakes of Whistler.

As we all know, Whistler was developed as a destination all-season resort, and a lot of people made their fortunes, but unfortunately, not Matt. In fact, Matt told us he was the only person known to be involved in the development of Whistler who left owing money, a lot of money. Sometimes these "gold rushes" just do not pan out. After dumping thirty thousand dollars into repairs on a Ford diesel pickup (why stop now?), it was time to pick up the stakes.

Matt was a lawyer and decided to move back with his family to California and take the California bar exam, but he needed money. We bought the windsurfer for the amount of the bar exam fee.

We put it on top of the neighbors VW van and brought it home. I can be seen windsurfing on Lake Union on the front page of the *Seattle Weekly* in 1985!

Bruce, a contractor who was remodeling a neighbor's house, arrived by boat each morning. Bruce had built the wooden boat and painted it green and yellow from paint leftover from various jobs. Bruce needed funds and warned us the boat needed "some work," but we bought another wooden boat anyway. It came with a motor, our first, but we were talking real money in those days and needed a partner.

Legal services in Seattle in the 1970s spawned a lot of friendships. Anne, the wife at the time of one of my husband's colleagues, was the perfect partner. Anne and I formed a 1970s Second Wave feminist support group, which evolved into a women's basketball team. None of us had ever played basketball, and we were too old to have benefited from the passage of Title IX in 1972, which protected against discrimination based on sex in education, including participation in sports. Community centers were organizing women's basketball, and our team found a sponsor, the rock group Heart. The truth is our team was terrible and we lost our first game forty-six to five. I still remember the other team yelling, "Help them, help them!" to their players on the court.

We toured all of Lake Union with our partner Anne in the old green and yellow boat. We repaired leaks as they developed, sometimes as we motored! But it was too much. For several months Anne sat with us on the houseboat and watched the boat rot. We used the boat to illustrate the verb tenses for "to sink" for our daughter: sink, sank (preterit), and sunk (past participle). The steering wheel stays attached to our deck fencing to this day and has served as a toy for a couple generations of tots.

Bruce, the contractor, went on to buy another bigger and better, but still wooden, cabin cruiser boat. On September 2, 1984, he brought it into our channel and tied up at Andy and Barb's (our neighbors) house. George and I took the plunge and were married on the boat with friends and family filling the channel in boats and watching from neighbors' decks. The wedding reception met the approval of my Greek in-laws: Greek food, Greek music, belly dancing, and a few extra runs for more retsina. The relationship has lasted for ten years of living together like hippies plus thirty-seven years of marriage, but the cabin cruiser sank a few months after the wedding.

Wedding invitation, 1984

Debby and George's wedding, Andy center (Universal Life Minister)

Our daughter was born in 1986, and there is ample documentation of her waterproofing. When she was ten, we bought a bright turquoise and white paddleboat, thinking it was safe and would be fun for her to use with friends. She would peddle to neighbors' houses (under watchful eyes), visit, and peddle back. We often said we felt the boat was safe for her because *it could not sink*.

One summer day, she and a friend got in the paddleboat and headed toward shore, like she had done many times. The routine was to peddle down and back, but as I looked down the waterway, they seemed to be stuck; they were standing in the boat and wildly gesturing. A couple of neighbors were out on their decks yelling and trying to pull them in. I canoed down to see why the rescue effort was underway.

The girls heard me say the boat was unsinkable. So they had taken a couple of buckets with them and were pouring water into the boat to see if they could make it sink! Prove us wrong! Once the boat was at water level, they could not maneuver it and were gripped by fear. They were at the shallow end of the waterway where they knew the Lake Union monster, which turned out to be an otter, lurked. I towed them back and they both learned how to bale a boat.

It turned out we were not done with wooden boats. There was one more, the "No Sea Um."

My husband's fishing buddy, Bass Bob, had bought an old houseboat in the late 1960s. He was known for his carpentry skills and a few personality quirks, including perfectionism. Although talented and funny, Bob had little interest in holding a job, which would only interfere with his multiple unfinished projects, including his house. He could never get anything done because: you could not do this without doing that first, and that could not be done until you did this, and so on. Bob was very backed up.

While we found this funny, his wife did not. Bob promised to find a job after he finished leveling his houseboat, which required him to work under the house in the crawl space between the log floatation and the house floor. (Most houseboats do not have this type of spacing.) One summer he spent two months, five to seven hours per day, prone under his house. By mid-August he appeared and announced he had successfully raised the houseboat two inches.

About this same time, Bob found a classic wooden boat for sale in Tacoma. We went down and looked at the boat in dry storage and agreed it was a classic. George and Bob bought the boat and trailered it to a newly rented garage in Seattle and began working to get the boat seaworthy. Several months of sanding and fiberglassing took place.

"Is the boat ready to go in the water?"

"No, we have to redo part of the hull."

"But it's the third time."

"Well, it isn't smooth enough yet."

I did not see (sea) the boat for six months and jokingly named it "No Sea Um" because I doubted the boat would ever see the sea!

We had been renting storage space for the boat with no end in sight. There was stress around money in Bob's marriage as well. In the divorce, Bob came up with the best rationale for spousal support that has ever been conjured: "My wife made a lot of money declaring me as a dependent all these years, and I think she should pay me back."

There was no chance for reconciliation and the boat had not seen daylight in over a year. The No Sea Um, which was by then seaworthy, was sold to an owner who did launch it.

Over the last few years, we have had two kayaks blow in, one orange and one blue. We tried to find the owners with neighborhood signs and providing Harbor Patrol with descriptions. No one claimed the kayaks, so they found a home with us. We had to figure out how to get in and out of the kayaks safely and dryly on a predictable basis. We do not understand how these gifts come, but they do. The kayaks are what we use the most now and are a respite from the pandemic. But that is not the end of the fleet. The kayaks float beside two paddleboards. Then there is the Trophy fishing boat and a small motor craft that belonged to a fishing buddy we also lost too soon, and we use it now for our granddaughter's boating lessons.

The houseboat is the hub binding the boats together. It has hosted polar bear parties, water ballet shows, fishing derbies, water basketball tournaments, and DOX parties for kids like the "It takes a village party" for Thea, David, and Lily. Can anyone count how many salmon have been barbecued here? And then, the Fourth of July parties. I can say we have shared the privilege of living here. Just as we do not know how any of this happened—none of it was planned—we do not always know how this way of living has changed others.

George teaching Brooke, 2019

Except for one, Carol.

I knew Carol for forty years. She found me through the research and advocacy work I was doing among homeless and exploited women and youth. I tried everything I could think of to help Carol, but in the early days of my research, we were not aware of post-traumatic stress and the long-term effects of multiple experiences with physical and sexual abuse from early childhood through yesterday. What we knew was that nothing worked, and we needed to figure out what was going on. Carol and I had a friendship and a simpatico that just went on. Once, she called me after a suicide attempt. I was afraid for her, and I recall telling her I did not know how to help her; she was going to have to try something else.

She kept at it and she eventually succeeded in her battle with addiction, married her "boyfriend" and moved to the coast, where she started an antique business and reunited with her children. Carol called me several times a year and wrote letters, always thanking me for saving her life. I never understood that because at the most critical times, I could not help. Finally, I asked her what it was that I had done and why she kept saying that I saved her life.

The next generation

"Well, you let me come to your house, the boats and all," she said. "I knew there was another way to live. You showed me there was another way to live, and I found another way to live for myself."

Carol enlightened me in many ways and helped me be more mindful of the marvel of water-living. Who knows what all happens to someone as they float on the water or move the water rowing, paddling, sculling, swimming—or when you just sit, look, and let the water move you?

We Slid into Yes
by Karen Lorene

We knocked on the door of a houseboat on Lake Union in Seattle.

A cheerful voice said, "Come in! We've been waiting for you. Sandy called."

We pushed the door open. And with that, we walked into a new life.

Our hosts sat on a large, cushioned sofa. "Make yourselves at home…upstairs, downstairs, be our guests. Look around," they said. They were relaxed, comfortable, and inviting. We thanked them for their hospitality. And so began our tour of houseboat #11.

What felt strange at the outset was that our host and hostess continued to sit in the front room as we headed toward the adjacent kitchen. It felt as if their staying seated was a way of "staging." It worked. The fourteen-hundred-square-foot home didn't seem small. By staying seated, our hosts made the space feel un-crowded and gracious. From their seats, they called out, "Room for all."

The kitchen was neat and tidy: butterscotch-colored tiles, polished oak floors, noon-day sun silhouetting on blossoming herbs. The appliances were full-sized: stove, double sink, dishwasher, microwave, and wine rack. Off to the side, tucked under a stairway to the second floor, was a generous pantry and the first of two bathrooms. Everything spoke of the owner's loves and likes, including the tomato-basil soup simmering on the stove. It was impossible to ignore its delicious smell.

Back in the living room, the owners waved us on to the upstairs bedroom. A wall of windows greeted us and gave us a full view of the Seattle skyline and Queen Anne Hill, and, of course, the Space Needle. Along another two walls were his closet and her closet, another bathroom, and white walls to be filled with our art collection. A last look at the skyline revealed neighbors busy hanging baskets of gloriously deep-red ruby geraniums. They waved a welcome, finished their planting, slipped into two lime-green kayaks, and paddled away.

Back downstairs, we headed to one last space occupied with computers, printers, rows of books, and a fold-down bed. Satisfied with our tour, we returned to the living room and thanked the owners and headed for the front door.

Don took my hand as we stepped outside. It took barely five minutes on the front porch to decide we had what we needed: two bedrooms, a bath and a half, a laundry room, and best of all, an upstairs view of the city we love. We lingered on the front porch, breathing in the fresh air blowing off Queen Anne Hill. Don beamed. I understood his expression. He asked, "Are you sure?"

"Positive," I answered.

We hugged, and without hesitation, we chimed, "Yes, let's do it," and knocked on the door for a second time.

You see, we had done our homework. First, we had noticed the newly posted "For Sale" signs along this slip of Lake Union. We determined one of the houseboats on the market was the one we had seen on last year's Houseboat Tour. Once a year, Seattle's houseboat community invites folks like us to view (and dream) of owning a houseboat. We had already begun to fall in love with that houseboat.

Friends helped too. Sandy, Don's oldest friend, had called. His voice had been full of urgency. "Sandy here," he said. "That houseboat you love—*your* houseboat—well, it's having an open house this afternoon. Get yourselves down here! I've already called the owners for a sneak preview. Come! Right now." Click. Sandy didn't wait to hear yes or no.

Without delay, Don grabbed my hand, and we were out the

door, down two blocks, to Sandy's houseboat on the same dock as the open house. We knocked on his door. He stepped outside and pointed down the dock. "There, number eleven. They are waiting for you!"

Sandy's words struck home. He kept talking as we headed down the dock. "I've told the owners about you. Don't wait, go. You won't regret it. You'll be the first to see it!"

We waved goodbye and kept walking. We soon understood Sandy's enthusiasm. For this very moment, we had a breathing space and only minutes before a hoard of "looky-loos" would follow us down the dock.

We knew houseboats could sell in a minute. Most did. Sandy's audacity was full of his awareness that houseboats sold—and sold quickly. Especially one as cute as #11. Truth? We weren't looking to move from our 1920s home just two blocks up the hill from Lake Union. We liked where we lived. We rented out four units in that house. We had little debt. But there we were, knocking on the door at #11.

"We're back," he called. "We'll take it." Three fateful words.

Surprise filled the owners' faces. They looked at each other. "Are you serious or simply crazy," they asked. They had thought we were joking. They hadn't mentioned price, dues, or closing dates.

What the owners didn't know was that we had called their broker just in case. We knew the price, the dues, and when they wanted to close. Our bank was ready. The market was ripe for the size of house we lived in, so it wouldn't be difficult to sell. We were in a good place financially. We were ready.

It wasn't the first time we had said yes to an experience. We had learned to define who we were and where we were without hesitation, ready for opportunities, openings, undefined possibilities, and crazy moments. We didn't expect to fall in love so easily. But? What was there not to like? It was magic.

"Why don't you come in for a glass of Chardonnay and a cup of tomato-basil soup," the owners said once they knew we were serious. "We have lots to talk about."

You see, dear reader, as if you didn't know already, the docks are magic, rich with plants that complement the joyous paint colors of houseboats: pea-green, tomato-red, sunshine-yellow, baby-blue. Every house shouts, "Hello!" And what's more, the colors are accompanied by the raucous greetings of large and small dogs bouncing from behind front doors. Even as we passed the waterway between two homes on the way to the open house, a dog toy flew through the air and a large collie hit the water with excitement. It was then we knew our puppy would be welcomed too.

It has now been eight years. Every wall inside and out of #11 has made room for our art. We don't know what our neighbors think of our choices. That is one of the wonders of houseboat living: everyone makes different choices resulting in an eclectic selection of color, shapes, and sizes of art. Color blasts out owner preferences. We are as different as our homes. We are as different as the front porches we share on warm, sunny afternoons, wine glass in hand, with our neighbors.

Someday, when the stairs are too much for old bodies, we will become "gifters." A couple will drop by for an open house. We will invite them in. They will fall in love with our house and style of living. They will stand on the front porch and say yes to a new and wonderous life.

The Perfect Day
by Samantha Skal

The year 2020 didn't have a lot of bright spots, but in late August during the COVID-19 lockdown, the universe delivered the type of Seattle summer day that I live for. After several months of lockdown and no outside social contact, this introverted extrovert was very ready for some socially distanced human interaction.

It was maybe four in the afternoon, ninety-seven degrees, dead calm, and not a cloud in the sky. Lake Union's water temperature was hovering in the low seventies, an annual peak us houseboaters look forward to all year. My husband and I lazily set out on our biggest paddleboard from the back deck, legs trailing in the water, a six-pack of a local session IPA in a dry bag in tow, and no particular plan in mind but to enjoy the hell out of the water and sun.

The lake was packed in the best possible way, with massive flotillas of socially distanced inflatable swans, flamingos, and donuts roped together and gently bouncing by groups of Canada geese, American coots, kayakers, SUPers, hot-tub boats, pristine white sailboats, rubber-walled dinghies, and the occasional large cruiser. The high use wasn't unusual for the time of COVID-19. That whole summer, mass rafts of floaties regularly bumped against our back dock, enjoying one of the only safe social activities available to lake-adjacent living: being on the water. Living in a houseboat with lots of windows can feel like a fishbowl at times, especially when strangers float by in your flooded backyard when you're on the couch on your fifth Zoom call of the day, but during Covid, it was a balm: interaction and proximity safely behind a wall of glass.

On this particular day, in the middle of the lake and the object of universal adoration, was an indestructible motorboat with three decks, the kind of well-loved vessel that looks like it's seen at least several thousand summer days. Its sides were a nondescript mix of peeling paint: pale-green, gray, baby-blue, and white. Woven rugs in bright colors, the kind I most closely associate as padding the floor of a dive bar's stage, were draped over the rails, giving the vessel a festive, Burning Man vibe. On the uppermost deck, a garage band had taken over, with a full drum set, a bass player, a guitar player, and a singer whose Hawaiian shirt was wet from multiple dives into the lake—fully clothed. Live music poured out of their ample speakers, drifting out over a three-hundred-sixty-degree crowd and spreading palpable joy. The musicians, who were belting out creative covers of Journey, The Eagles, Sublime, Def Leppard and The Stones' greatest hits, were as loud as they were enthusiastic.

We joined the smiling fray, ecstatic to just be there, to be a part of the unbridled joy that accompanies live rock music, especially in a year when everything was canceled. We cracked a beer just as the lead singer trailed off mid-song and said, "I forgot the words. Oh well!" and laughed.

It was the best concert I've ever seen.

We drifted around for what felt like hours, making friends, laughing, and having the same conversation over and over: what a joy of a day to be alive, to be on the lake, to be a part of this perfect day. How COVID-19 royally sucked, but how grateful it made us all for the little things we no longer had access to from Before, things like a cold beer on a hot day at an outdoor concert, hugging Gramma, or a lively dinner at a restaurant with good wine and good friends.

The evening came on, and the crowd thinned out, leaving only fifty or so fans listening to the band, who were now pushing up on an impressive four-hour set. If anything, the cheers and claps after each song were louder than with the larger crowd, the band

and the remaining floating fans holding tightly to the magic of the moment, not wanting it to end.

As the sun started to set, the heat of the day shifted into something anticipatory, the moisture building and leaving our skin dewy, the smell of fresh rain and ozone warring with the sunbaked marsh scent of the lake. Thunderstorms in Seattle are somewhat of a rarity, only hitting the city a few times a year and always cause for great excitement, at least for me. I love a good thunderstorm: the way they blow through quickly and violently, sometimes with hail, sometimes with rainbows. They force you to be in the present, demanding your attention and your awe. On this most perfect of days, as the band forgot the words to yet another song, and it was not annoying in the slightest, the sky took on the color of a too-ripe peach, burnt-yellow around the edges, and a dark cloud rolled in from the west. We watched it billow, the dark-gray mixing with the oranges, pinks, and lavenders, creating a perfect dream of a sunset.

Then, without warning, a flash of lightning arced across the sky, followed immediately by a crack of thunder that vibrated my chest like standing too close to a subwoofer at full volume. Being on the water in a thunderstorm is not the most ideal of scenarios, to put it mildly, and that vulnerable paddle back to the houseboat was one of my most energetic—ever. Hearts racing at the danger and being in the presence of such an awesome amount of energy, the second we were safe inside, we flung the back doors wide open, and without bothering to dry off, we watched the storm rip through, warm rain bouncing off the deck and onto our sun-kissed skin, grins a mile wide.

There's nothing quite like witnessing a summer storm while living on the water. You can feel the impact of the wind even while inside because the house rocks and your pendant lights swing. The rain sweeps across the water, and you can see it coming by the way the water gets churned up and changes color, from a dark-blue to a pale-gray. The sound the wind-churned waves make when they hit the house is one of my favorite sounds in the world, a sound best described as "blerp."

This storm was deafening, wet, thrilling, and over within twenty minutes. As it rolled east, it left behind a once-again placid lake, and air that smelled like a promise of a brighter future, sparkling clean and earth-scented. Rainwater dripped off the roof and into the lake with pleasingly soft plops, combining with the chortles of the ever-present wood ducks, and in the distance, a final drum solo.

It was a perfect day in a wildly imperfect year.

The author on the lake on another summer day in 2020, in front of another common lake denizen, the gravel barge.

Lake Union Monster

by Sally Macdonald

The little duck was there. Until it wasn't.

It shimmied to shed the water from its latest dive just beyond our neighbor Bob's deck as Bob trained his new video camera that way.

Then…a splash, a shocked quack, and a flurry of feathers before the water settled back into a lazy ripple.

We houseboaters began referring to the events of that afternoon as THE DAY THE LAKE UNION MONSTER ATE THE DUCK IN FRONT OF BOB'S VIDEO CAMERA.

Bob's video of a beast from the deep—shown only as a blurry maw breaking the surface of the water—made the local news for several days.

Then most of Seattle went back to summer as usual.

But we in our houseboat community took to thinking we heard weighty splashes in the water off our decks.

Melanie thought a big man cannonballed off her back deck one afternoon. *Probably just a river otter that had done its business between the potted plants on her deck*, someone scoffed. Or a giant bass. *There's supposed to be a ten-pounder out there in the water*, someone else claimed. *Maybe it was a sea lion that swam through the locks from Puget Sound to grift freshwater goodies from our lake*, I ventured.

No one had the guts to wonder out loud if it was actually THE MONSTER THAT ATE THE DUCK IN FULL VIEW OF BOB'S NEW VIDEO CAMERA THE OTHER DAY.

Yeah, well, all that has happened before, said the state wildlife guy we called out of curiosity.

Any one of those could have been Bob's monster, he shrugged as if it really didn't matter.

After that, we all tried to go on about our lives in spite of Bob's duck-eating monster and the mysterious happenings occurring ever since it appeared. But every time we looked at the murky green water off our decks, we were well aware that whatever it was, was still out there.

Ours is one of about 500 houseboats in Seattle. Most of them are tethered side-by-side on long docks that protrude like fingers around the perimeter of our in-city lake.

We houseboaters like to think of ourselves as somehow different from other Seattleites. Most of us don't mind announcing to the tourists who sometimes wander down to check out this novel way of living that we are a charming anomaly within the city.

Our houseboat is about the size of a double-wide, but many are as big as any land house. Houseboaters tend to paint their places every color in nature and decorate them with wind chimes and all sorts of other hanging gewgaws.

A neighbor who was trying to learn how to create Northwest Native art painted a red otter on the front of our house. Melanie used to have so many potted plants that her place looked like a grow operation. Peter's bright-red house is festooned with Mexican clay art.

Our houses are about an oar's distance from each other, so we sit within a casual "how's it going" from the floating homes on either side of us. And we share our watery world with more wild things than a landlubber might think.

So we thought it was important to know WHAT THE HECK KIND OF MONSTER BOB CAUGHT ON CAMERA THAT DAY. And we didn't mind pressing the state wildlife guy for more than a shoulder shrug and a "yeah, well."

The fact that we would spend a considerable amount of time

discussing the possibility of sharing an afternoon swim with such a fiend still on the lam is understandable. As far as we can tell, anyway.

You shouldn't think we on our houseboat dock have nothing more to talk about than BOB'S LAKE UNION MONSTER. There are plenty of other critters in our water to focus on.

Some of my neighbors doubt it, but I can tell you the season by looking at whatever fish or fowl is out there in the water off our deck.

Melanie could do that too.

In late summer, there's a coho salmon run through the lake into the creeks and mountain streams that feed it. That's when the Muckleshoot Indians, who have native rights to fish the lake, uncoil their gill nets to take advantage. One year we helloed out to one of the boats and the fishermen came over to sell us the freshest salmon you can get, straight out of the water, still gasping.

We know it's winter when the sky and the lake cast a leaden countenance on our lake and winds from the north whip it into whitecaps. We houseboaters spend much of the winter hunkered down inside, waiting out the dark and cold while many of our animal neighbors nap.

Bob was the only one of us who spent much time that winter thinking about his FAMOUS DUCK-EATING MONSTER. Every time we'd run into him on the way to the mailboxes out by the street, he would bore us to distraction, bragging about how he had been in just the right place at just the right time.

That's not to say the lake isn't busy in winter. That's when the diving ducks—goldeneyes and buffleheads with their black-and-white tuxedo plumage and mergansers with their scraggly ducktail hairdos—fly in to escape the Alaska weather, joining the cormorants for a fresh-water fishing season. Occasionally the birds forget we may be watching and venture into our channel for lunch.

Sometimes in the fall and winter, when I am reading in my perch near the window, I catch a blur of startling white shoot past our house and down the waterway toward shore.

The first year it happened, the neighbors quit fretting about THE MONSTER BOB CAUGHT ON HIS CAMERA EATING A DUCK IN ONE GULP and took to haggling about what kind of bird it could be. It had the spindly legs, hunched-over stance, and spear-like beak of a heron, but we'd never seen anything like it before. Its dazzling white color clearly told us it wasn't a heron.

That bird looks like an ibis, said someone who reads a lot but was just guessing. *Looks like a cattle egret to me*, said a neighbor from the Midwest who used to see them perched on the backs of cows out in the field, feeding on the bugs that were feeding on the cows.

But most of us—and my bird book agrees—said it was a great egret.

We're at the very northern edge of the egret's range, so we are wowed anew every winter when it comes back to visit with its cousin, a great blue heron that hangs about our dock year-round. They're like old buddies whose favorite fishing hole is the shallows near shore where the milfoil shelters a good catch of minnows.

Spring is the most active time of year on our docks. That's when we houseboaters start cleaning up whatever winter left behind, filling our decks with flowerpots and catching up on the neighborhood gossip.

We notice then—it happens suddenly and unexpectedly—

that the migratory birds have flown off, back to their Arctic summer homes.

About the same time, the Canada geese, who have been speechless all winter, begin squawking off-key love calls and stomping around on our rooftops looking for an empty flowerpot to lay eggs in. It's a raucous dating scene.

We use all kinds of tricks every spring to keep lovelorn mallards and Canada geese, who live here all year, from using our planters as bassinets. If they lay eggs on your deck, you might not be able to get out the back door for weeks until the hatchlings are ready to swim out into the wider world. If you get too close to their babies, the geese don't hesitate to run at you, hissing and spitting.

So we try to scare the geese and ducks off if they even look like they might commandeer our back decks for a nursery.

One day I was gazing out our window toward the water when I caught a glimpse of Bob pushing a flowerpot off his deck into the lake.

A single egg floated away among the dirt and peat moss as Bob caught me staring at him. He came running over to explain he hadn't had a chance to plant his flowers yet and the geese had laid the egg in the flowerpot on his deck—and we can't have that.

I could see Bob felt a little guilty. I was sorry I saw him dump the egg. But I was also sorry I didn't get to watch it hatch on his deck.

When the geese came back from their outing that afternoon, they were furious. They honked and hollered and flew at Bob, driving him into the house. When they saw him peeking at them from the kitchen window, they attacked, flying at the glass and banging their beaks against it and making a terrible racket. They kept it up for days. Every time they saw Bob trying to sneak past the window, he was fair game.

And you can believe this or not, although I saw it, so I know it's true: those geese came back again the next nesting season, honking and flying at Bob's house, even though he had sold it to Kit by then and moved away.

Eventually the geese gave up trying to punish Bob for pushing their egg into the water. But they haven't tried to raise a family on that deck since.

About the same time the geese and ducks start looking to raise a family, our closest wild neighbors, the raccoons, begin to wake up from their pseudo hibernation and tend to the babies that were born while we weren't paying attention.

The raccoons have spent the winter napping in messy comfort in nests they arrange in the few inches of space between our flotation rafts and our floorboards.

If you listen very early in the morning in spring, you can hear the mama raccoons taking the kids out for a walk down the dock, chattering away to keep them in line. Sometimes the little ones fall overboard and the mamas have a terrible time getting them out of the water and back up on the dock.

Most people who live on land think the raccoons are cute, and I guess they are. But most people don't have to live as close to them as we do, and they're not always the best of neighbors.

For as many years as I can remember, a bunch of raccoons made their nests under the stairs leading from Bev's kitchen to her living room. They caused an awful stink and, being nocturnal, made an awful racket when Bev was trying to sleep.

We've heard the raccoon families under our bedroom too, scooting about for a more comfortable sleeping position or coughing softly in the night.

Once, a couple of raccoons had a row in our waterway after midnight, screaming and acting like they'd like to drown each other. Eventually they called a draw, and we all went back to bed.

Bev finally had enough. She called the pest-control people, who did their best. But when generations of raccoons decide to hand down a prime nesting spot like it's a family estate, they aren't easy to evict.

Over time we have learned to treat the raccoons like the wild things they are.

We had no choice when some of the raccoon families began attacking people as they took their dogs out for walks.

The neighbors were horrified.

Bob may have moved away, but this was much, much scarier than THE MONSTER THAT ATE THE DUCK RIGHT IN FRONT OF HIS VIDEO CAMERA.

During one attack, one of the neighbors beat the raccoons off with a golf club. Someone else grabbed her purse to help and was also attacked. Several people and their pets were injured badly enough to need stitches and rabies shots.

So we called the wildlife officials in again.

It looked like maybe some of the mama raccoons had gone rogue and were teaching their kids to go after us. The official wildlife guy allowed us to watch as he set a trap in the flower bed we cared for on shore.

But stalking people and pets like a wolf pack is not a hunting style for raccoons that I know of, he said to those of us gathered around to watch.

He winked when he told us he was going to cart the offenders off to a new home in the mountains. Some of the neighbors said later they believed him. I saw him wink, though, and I really don't think he was taking those bad boys anywhere this side of heaven.

When the weather turned nice that year, we considered whether we should swim off our decks again. We seemed to have dealt with the rogue raccoons and all, but the Lake Union Monster was still out there.

I thought I'd pass. I didn't think A MONSTER THAT WOULD EAT A WHOLE DUCK RIGHT IN FRONT OF BOB would hesitate to take a bite out of a swimmer.

And we've had other run-ins with nature over the years.

For instance, there's the beaver that roams the neighborhood at night, looking for building materials for a dam or fresh greens for breakfast.

Once I decided a willow tree would be a beautiful addition to a spot on the east side of our house. Willows grow well in the lake water, but you do have to tie the trunk to the house or dock to keep them upright and wrap the base with chicken wire to protect them from the beaver.

One morning we discovered a limb from the four-foot sapling we'd planted was gone, chewed off at the trunk. The next day, another limb went missing.

Apparently we hadn't been generous enough with the chicken wire. All the beaver had to do was balance on the edge of the deck, stretch a little and, voila—breakfast, lunch, and dinner for a week.

Last summer, he ate the apple tree we neighbors grew in a planter up on land. For years running, Bev had won first prize in the pie-baking contest with apples from that tree. And now the beaver had whittled it down to a stub.

Despite the loss of our apple tree, our dismay at how the raccoons turned delinquent on us, our joy at the egret's annual visit, and our continued quarrels with the aquatic critters who live among us, we neighbors pretty much agree it's best to give them all a pass when their natural instincts take over.

A long time ago, when we were debating WHAT COULD

HAVE EATEN THE DUCK RIGHT IN FRONT OF BOB'S VIDEO CAMERA, someone suggested that the great pink maw that opened and swallowed a mallard whole that day might belong to a beaver.

Probably not, the state wildlife official said when we brought it up with him again.

Actually, I think a river otter is your villain, he said. *They eat lots of things you might not think they'd eat if you live on land. Fish, frogs, that sort of thing.*

Then last summer, the plumber-diver we hired to do some dock work said the very same thing when we asked his opinion.

(Some of the workmen we hire have to have multiple talents to work out here on the water, hence the plumber-diver.)

We had called him about some problems we were having with the pipes that bring city water out to us on the dock. He pried up a board that runs down the center of our dock and saw, on the logs that provide flotation for it, thousands of fresh-water clam shells.

The clams live on the bottom of the lake, the plumber-diver explained, *and river otters think they're delicious*. They use the logs that serve as flotation for the dock as dinner tables and leave the shells there.

I think an otter ate your duck too, the plumber-diver said with a confidence that came from the fact that his wife was a marine biologist. *She said they also eat ducks sometimes.*

Some of the neighbors are doubtful.

We'd kind of hate to actually solve the riddle of the Lake Union Monster that has preoccupied us for years. We've always sort of enjoyed tossing it around amongst us.

But who are we to argue with the plumber-diver's wife?

A little later, I heard the two Otter Brothers who live under the marina nearby calling to each other, right off our deck, early in the morning. It's how they keep track of each other, an insistent high-pitched cry, kind of a combination yip-hoot that humans might ignore but otters cannot.

I went out on the deck, and there they were, swimming right up to me, staring up from the water with eyes as big and sweet as chocolate drops.

Not at all like MONSTERS THAT WOULD EAT A WHOLE DUCK RIGHT IN FRONT OF BOB OR GOD OR ANYONE, leaving behind nothing but ripples and tail feathers.

"How could you." I sighed. "That poor little duck."

The Dog Interview
by Darla Adams, with John S. Adams

When I was a six-month-old pup, a curious and frightening event occurred. My Peeps, the humans who feed me, decided to live in a floating home at the end of a long dock over the water. They were asked: "Did you know your dog needs to be interviewed?"

The humans do not need to be interviewed to live in a floating home, but waggers like me do. On the big day, my Peeps and I cautiously walked down the dock and stepped onto the deck of a floating home with colorful flower boxes and the aroma of lavender. The interviewer, Kim, was a top corporate attorney. She had a very sweet dog, we were told, but this was not a dog-to-dog interview. Those are easy—nose to nose, nose to tail, turn around, do-si-do.

Kim had a different idea. She started out with human pleasantries, making my Peeps comfortable in her tidy, bright-blue, one-story floating home. I smelled a cat, which made me nervous. And a dog, which made me excited. And then Kim turned to me, with her corporate-attorney steely eyes, and asked directly, "Does she bark?" I wanted to bite her but didn't.

With a nervous wag, I decided to engage in being sheepish and ducked my head, avoiding confrontation. The attorney was relentless. "Does she chase other dogs? How much training has she had?"

My Peeps carefully answered, hoping beyond hope that they could run this gauntlet without being told their home deposit was being refunded.

The moment came when Kim's dog came out from under the sofa. With all the power in my paws, I lunged. "Arrff! Arrf! Arrf!" Enthusiasm overwhelmed diplomacy, and I started to jump off my girl Peep's lap. Just a sniff! Just a wag!

"Just a moment," my girl human said as she turned me around and tucked me into her lap. Foiled!

Apparently not noticing the crisis averted, Kim was in the process of explaining that this dock had a prohibition against Dobermans, pit bulls, and mean dogs. Then the tea was finished, I was offered a dog bone, and my owners left with hearts in the air. The dog interview was over.

Life settled down after I was accepted, and my owners were allowed to live in the floating home community. Since our yard is blue instead of green, and far out from the lakeshore, my Peeps got me a "pet pad," which is a piece of grass in a box that gets changed every week. It was hard to get used to, but I do go out on the deck on my pad. When out there on the porch, I watch the rowing crews swish past our home and the roaring float planes swoop and land on the water.

On early morning walks, many visitors come to the dock. The first one I saw was a gleaming black otter that smelled like old fish. She noticed me, hissed loudly, and slid into the water. Once I saw a deer that came far out on the dock and ate petunias from a flower box. Raccoons are here, with tiny black hands that seem like human hands, darting into the ripples and holding a fish. And a great blue heron, with a giant needle nose, also comes to fish, hopping from one houseboat deck to another.

Sometimes big boats will speed by our home, and the waves make me dizzy as the house rocks from side to side. When the waves are too big, the floating home floor slants to one side, which makes it fun to chase my toys. However, my Peeps have to hire divers to go under the house and blow up the air tank to make it level again. The divers always come to the door first, and I race down the stairs to meet them. "Arrff, arrff, arff! You will *diiiiie!*" I warn, but they are good to dogs. They pat me on the head, and I lick their hands and decide not to kill them today.

There are many types of boats that can hold a dog on Lake Union. The rowboats can hold a golden retriever. A canoe can hold three springer spaniels. A common site here is a bulldog on the back of a paddleboard. Elegant yachts with a greyhound look fine, but they do not have happy dogs. Those boats are noisy, and the dogs are far above the water where they cannot sniff. By far the most appealing to me is the green kayak.

When I first saw my Peeps get into it, I did not suspect my fate. The lady who sold my humans the floating home gave them a bottle of champagne and a dog life vest. It was meant to be a nice present, but I have never shivered and quaked as much as when I thought they might throw me in the water. Once they put the vest on me, they did just that. I held my breath and paddled and paddled with my eyes bugging out, panting hard. When they pulled me up to the deck, I had a fine revenge and shook a huge arc of water all over them. All three of us had to towel off. They laughed and I barked.

Once they were sure I could swim with the life vest on, we could go out in the green kayak every sunny afternoon. At first I thought I would be thrown in, and I shivered and quaked. But when I was put up in the front of the hatch, snug and dry and could fly into the warm wind, I found a new calling. The green kayak is now my friend, and it's always a good day when my humans put the life vest on and we go for a paddle on the lake.

My Peeps sometimes run out of fermented grape juice, so we

all go to Pete's Market for more. That is the place to meet all the dogs in the neighborhood. They are all shapes and sizes, and all the dogs have a human they take on walks. On the way to Pete's, I pull hard on the leash because my Peeps are so slow. We need to get to the grass by the park! That is where all the dogs mark, and I can tell which dogs were there, if they are healthy, and who is in heat. I sniff and sniff, which is how I learn the daily dog news. My humans call that "reading the *New York Times*." We usually take a long walk, looking at the boats and ducks and squirrels, talking to other dogs and their people.

Once they get their fermented grape juice and come home, my Peeps often go up the spiral stairs to the roof deck without me. I am not sad, because it is too scary up there. They say it is the third story of our home, but it has no ceiling and no walls, so a dog could fall off. I went up once, and it has a big flat roof, umbrellas, and some iron furniture that won't blow away in a windstorm. They sit up there for hours with their friends, laughing and watching the sun set.

One time of year, everything is very noisy and exciting. The Fourth of July is a time when thousands of people come from far away to visit their friends on the lake and sit on the shore and the roof decks of the floating homes. A barge is brought into the middle of the lake and they practice making explosions. It is a hard time for dogs, as we hear every firework all around the lake. I am very brave, unlike my friend Bria next door. She is a beautiful golden retriever with soft, sensitive ears, who tries to crawl under the rug with every "boom!"

My Peeps invite many friends to go up to the roof deck on that day. I meet them and wag and jump, as I know them all and they all love me. Then they bring all their stinky human food and fermented drinks up to the roof, and I go into my safe dog cave with the Pendleton blanket. As it gets dark, they listen to the "1812

Overture" played over loudspeakers and "Ooh!" and "Ahh!" as giant explosions, brightly colored lights, and clouds of gunpowder fill the skies.

After the Fourth of July, it gets warm, and the lake becomes very busy. There are hundreds of pleasure craft moored all around the lake. Many are tied up to floating homes and have dogs I can only see and sniff in the summer when their owners go out on their boats. The boaters shed most of their clothing and sail, motor, ski, row, and paddle to show off and meet one another. One thing I always notice with the humans is that if they are quiet, somber, or grumpy on land. When they get out on the water, their eyes light up, laughter comes into their voices, and they are the happiest you can ever see a human.

Some things I see on the water I cannot explain. Every Tuesday, hundreds of sailboats go zig-zagging around a course on the lake doing what my Peeps call the "Duck Dodge." Some summer afternoons we see little round boats shaped like donuts with drinks in the middle that people paddle with their feet. In all types of weather, groups of almost-naked college students go by in a floating hot tub powered by a wood-burning stove. Quiet electric boats flow by in the evenings with tinkling glasses and meals served on linen tablecloths.

We have many smells in the summer. The humans barbecue on their decks and invite each other over, talking and talking. The smell of roasting salmon and meat in the air can drive a dog crazy, and we sometimes howl to each other from dock to dock. The humans can't bury their scraps because we live over water, so they use a wagon for the compost, trash, and recycling, which they sort and pull from the dock to land. When we walk by the bin with the food compost, I inhale deeply. It all smells good to me.

Being a dog on a floating home is good because there are so many delivery people. They come with packages, envelopes, and pizzas. Each one is a barking opportunity for all the dogs on the dock. At the head of the dock by the parking lot, Sophie the mini poodle sounds the alarm. As the delivery person comes down the dock, Kim's Havanese, Stogie, sounds off from her blue house, then Miss Darcy, a spinster terrier, then Bella next door, then Bria, the beautiful retriever across the dock from our home. That is the signal for me to begin.

I am a big help, spinning around and warning, "Arrf, arrf," to break eardrums as the package lands on the front step. My Peeps say I don't need to be so worried, because bad people who are caught trying to steal would have to jump in the water to try to get away. Then the harbor police could scoop them out of the cold water in their big boat with the loudspeaker. But guarding is my job. I

may only weigh three bricks, but I am fierce, and I am part of the floating-home-dog-pack security alert system.

We have a famous dog on our dock. Maddie is an elegant Spinone and has her own book. She is twenty times as big as me, with long, orange, roan hair. Her owner thinks she is the very best dog in the world. So, I sometimes wonder, am I a good dog also? Then I remember that I passed the dog interview.

The Mindset and Mechanics of Apologies
by Mary M. Mitchell

Have you ever walked down any of the floating home docks? Quite possibly, the answer is no, since most prominently display "No Trespassing" signs at the point of entry. Others feature locked gates. Most can be viewed from vantage points along the bordering thoroughfares. And from that vantage point, you will have to admit that these houses, especially the vintage ones, are a quirky lot.

Imagine, then, the differing personalities of those who inhabit these spaces.

Indeed, some are outgoing, everlastingly cheerful, almost Pollyanna types. Others are curmudgeonly, and some are hermits, hardly, if ever, to be seen by another human being. All are, in their own way, rugged individualists. Much like the houses they inhabit.

Imagine, if you can, what a disagreement between any of these rugged individualists might look like.

What might be the source of said disagreement? It may well be about water rights for their kayak, canoe, paddleboard, rowboat, sailboat, powerboat, or raft. It could have something to do with sight lines—as owners remodel, put on second floors, bring in new homes to the old float, tear down and rebuild. It could be about noise. Sounds do travel better (or worse, as the case may be) over water. Fireplace smoke can create health risks for some, while neighbors blatantly choose to ignore that.

Dogs can be an issue. Cats, too. Some leave food out for raccoons. Others leave trash on their porches.

The point is that disagreements occur, as in any neighborhood, although the causes in the floating home community may be a bit different and the personalities involved a bit quirkier. Heated arguments, hurt feelings, insults, shunning, ends of beautiful friendships—any of these consequences are possible.

What to do? Apologize. But how to do it constructively is the question.

One of my most influential teachers said, "If you want to learn anything in this life, if you want to become the person God meant you to be, you must be willing to be wrong." He is also the guy who taught me that, if I want to change anything, it means changing myself first. This means not copping out and blaming anyone or anything else when things don't go as they should—or more to the point, when they don't go *my* way.

For example, the day when I sat around waiting for an appliance delivery that never came. Daylight hours are at a premium, and sunlight is rarer in early February. I found my temper getting the best of me as I called the dealership, barely able to mind my manners. Which in my field is exactly what is expected of me—at all times and under all circumstances.

"I have been waiting all day for this refrigerator, and my dog can't hold it any longer."

"Why haven't you taken him out, ma'am? Your delivery is scheduled for tomorrow."

Certainly, I could have disputed this fact. After all, I had it down in my calendar. Yet I have been known, once or twice at the most, to get the day wrong. So I simply said, "I am terribly sorry for my sharp words. This was my mistake. I will be more careful in the future and double check the dates." In my humblest voice.

And, what do you know? They delivered the refrigerator the following day, as scheduled, installed it for free, and patiently showed me how to manage all the controls.

OWN UP TO THE TRUTH

It's so easy to take somebody else's inventory and conclude that they are completely self-delusional. It's also simple, yet not easy, to see that in ourselves.

Who wants to be wrong? Certainly not me. It seems, however, that I bungle things a lot. Big things and little things. But if I own up to causing the problem, don't blame it on anybody else or on circumstances, and apologize for whatever hurt feelings or losses I might have caused, whatever the magnitude of my errors, people are far more likely to forgive me and move on.

It takes courage to apologize and mean it. When we apologize, we are holding ourselves accountable to the truth. It also requires compassion to apologize. To do this, we need to put ourselves in the other person's shoes and feel how they feel as a result of our perceived misdeed. A true apology takes a bit of reflection; not just a knee-jerk "I'm sorry."

Sorry is a state of being, as in "What a sorry old kayak you have there." On the other hand, to apologize is an action. Apologies without action are as shallow as rainwater on a leaky floating home roof.

There is something sacred about apologizing. Especially when we realize—and accept—that a true apology carries with it the appropriate amends. If we're not going to do something differently and thus heal the situation, our apology is dishonest. Apologies are sacred because they help clear the path to moving forward in life after we've fallen and picked ourselves up again.

In fact, sometimes the experience of "going to the fire" with a neighbor and making amends actually creates a stronger bond.

Knowing how and when to apologize is invaluable. It relieves stress, diminishes resentment, and paves the path for progress.

THE MECHANICS OF APOLOGY

So, you goofed. We all do. The question now is what are you going to do about it?

That, of course, depends on the magnitude of the goof. One thing is certain. You must say it in words, and perhaps even with flowers or chocolate or some other gift. Muffins for the appliance delivery guy might not have been appropriate, but I did thank the appliance dealership person who fielded my call for being so understanding. And I called him by name, because I always make an effort to remember the name of the person to whom I am speaking.

Bless the immediacy of technology! However, texts, breezy emails, and charmingly Jurassic telephone calls simply are not enough. When the goof is particularly painful, write a letter of apology.

WRITING A LETTER OF APOLOGY: THE SSA FORMULA

SSA stands for Specificity, Significance, Action. It is my foolproof SSA formula for writing letters of apology. This formula also works when composing letters of thanks, condolence, or congratulations.

First, admit that what you said or did was wrong and that you truly are sorry for having done it. Be specific. For example, "I apologize for yelling at your contractor yesterday," is better than a bland, "I'm sorry about yesterday."

Second, emphasize that there was no excuse for what you did. Yet, if you feel you must, note any mitigating circumstances. Then acknowledge what your actions cost the other person in terms of time, energy, hurt feelings, etc. That's the significance. For example, "I could kick myself for blowing my stack when it was raining cats and dogs and your guys were just trying to protect your place."

Third, say how you will make sure never to repeat your gaffe and mention whatever reasonable ideas come to mind for rectifying the damage you've caused. That's the action. For example, "I hope you know that I've learned a valuable lesson from this unfortunate incident. In the future, I'll remember that we're all in this floating home community together, looking out for each other, contractors included."

WHAT AN APOLOGY MEANS

Remember to speak in terms of observable behavior and its effects. In other words, you can apologize for hurting someone's feelings with your sharp comments, but that doesn't necessarily mean that you are apologizing for what you think and feel. An apology does mean that you are repentant for the effects of your behavior on someone else. It means that you will change your behavior and not repeat your slight.

When we were kids, our parents used to reproach us to "take things back" when we said something wrong. If only life were that easy.

Here is a classic example of this:

At one point, when my husband was serving as president of our cooperative, a letter, which was written in anger and was not factually accurate, was circulated to all owners. A series of unwarranted allegations was made, among others that a non-compliance notification with respect to required fireplace inspections was too rudely delivered. Harassment was claimed, and the writer called for removal of my husband from his voluntary position. After any number of neighbors spoke out against the allegations, the instigator came over and apologized, admitting that he was incorrect in what he said and wrong to have written such a letter in anger.

The apology was accepted. More importantly, there followed a letter of apology and retraction to the whole community. Hurt feelings were avoided, my husband was elected to a second term, and the whole incident blew away with no significant repercussions.

FROM THE OTHER SIDE

Accept apologies. Be gracious and sincere. Otherwise, you will undo the good in the experience. Obviously, if someone assassinates your character, steals your money and your spouse, this advice is not necessarily for you. Generally, though, authentically accepting someone's apology goes a long way toward forgiveness on both sides.

Here is another example, this from our own experience:

When we first moved into the community, we celebrated by dancing joyfully in the kitchen to the strains of Paul Simon's "Me and Julio Down by the Schoolyard," with the volume pumped way up. We turned off our new Bose system and headed off to work, only to receive a phone call eight hours later asking us to please turn down the volume.

Apparently, our stereo had been blasting Paul Simon and five other CDs over and over. We found several notes tacked to our door, some more polite than others. Our apology was made at the community board meeting the following night, when we found out that one of our neighbors had the same system and that, in turning his on and playing it all day, he had in fact unknowingly also turned ours back on!

The significance of this snafu was obvious and apparent to the whole neighborhood and therefore did not need to be re-hashed. The action, of course, was to reprogram the remote.

And all was well, until the next dust-up.

More than We'd Bargained For
by Jim Weber

We bought our floating home on a gorgeous fall day from K.R., a single woman who was rather reluctant to sell. Which is surprising since most of the other people who had lived there previously, including many of our neighbors, moved on as soon as possible to another floating home, to a retirement community—anywhere to avoid the disadvantages of the place, most notably the tendency to tilt.

An enterprising couple had tried to address this problem by floating in an orphaned log, probably illegally, likely under the cover of night. K.R. undid whatever benefit came from affixing the purloined log by putting a number of file cabinets on the second floor, by which time there was little room for anything else, owing to the presence of a monstrous sofa.

The myriad of folks who have lived in our home remember this sofa. Nobody had any idea how long it had been there, or how it could have been installed on the second floor. Any thoughts of taking it out had been squelched by the apparent impossibility of accomplishing the task.

Bringing in overstuffed file cabinets necessitated adding air barrels to the scads of Styrofoam under the home. This kept it afloat for all but the winter months, when the Army Corps of Engineers lowered the water level. During those months, the home teetered to and fro while mired in the mud. But this we did not know on the day we signed the papers and took possession.

"And you can keep the nice leather couch in the living room."

"Thank you," we told the seller—politely—because my wife, Mary, is a leading authority on etiquette, and because we looked at it as part of the cost of doing business with K.R. Besides, we figured that anything that had been brought in must have been removable. That is, until we took measurements. We began to think that the second floor must have been built around the sofa.

In taking ownership, we were well aware that the bathroom was tiny and that the built-in bed could be accessed from one side only. Fortunately, we both are fitness instructors and capable of contorting ourselves as needed. We asked an artist friend what could be done with the bathroom. Her solution was to "expand it" via huge floor-to-ceiling vistas of a jungle, replete with leopards, a frog, a river, and dense forestation.

About that bed… It was built into the side of the bedroom and in an odd shape: too narrow and too long for any conventional mattress. We found the foam slab that came with the purchase to be only slightly less obsolete than the sofa and ordered a custom mattress. Finding sheets was difficult enough, but making the bed was something else.

As a yoga teacher, especially as a younger man, I was able to insinuate myself against the wall and under the slanted ceiling as we pulled the mattress out. By dint of nearly back-breaking effort, aided with prayers and imprecations, we somehow managed to change the sheets, albeit as seldom as possible.

As the weather started turning colder and the skies grayer, our artist friend suggested warmer, brighter colors for the interior. The house painter, facing the daunting task of working around the nine-foot eyesore of a sofa, came up with a novel proposal.

"I think I can get that sofa out," he offered to my surprise.

"You can't do it. I measured it—the narrow stairway and the doors. Even if we could somehow get it out the door and onto the porch, it's far too heavy to lower over the balcony to the dock."

"My friend has a chain saw."

And so, out it went. In four pieces.

We were getting by, that is, until winter set in, whereupon the floating home got stuck in the mud, and the wind came whistling through the walls. Even with baseboard heaters cranked up to the max, we slept in sweaters, long johns, night caps, and wool socks.

On one memorable night I got out of the only side of the bed that afforded an exit (Mary volunteered for the side against the wall, described to all her friends as "the pneumonia hole," which invariably caused them to level an unmistakable stink eye in my general direction), only to find the ambient indoor temperature a bone-chilling fifty-one degrees, not counting the wind-chill factor.

The log poachers walked by the next morning as I was doing jumping jacks, hoping to restart my circulation. "How are you coping during this cold snap?"

I tried to say, "Terribly," but my teeth were chattering so much that I think they must have thought I said, "Tolerably."

"That's good," one of them said as they smiled and strolled on.

Two months and two portable space heaters later, and thawed out enough to attempt meaningful conversation, I asked them if they had any idea why our place was so cold.

"Oh, it has no insulation, other than newspapers."

"Well, that's a fine how-de-doo. K.R. never told us that."

"When we lived in your place, just long enough to enclose the back porch, we pulled old newspapers out of the walls, some of them still legible and dating back to 1913."

That day, I went out and bought a mattress heater, which probably saved our lives—and our marriage. That did it. We decided to do a big remodel.

The first-floor walls were bumped out in four places. This would afford us: more counter and eating space in the kitchen; a bigger bedroom with a centrally located bed; an enlarged bathroom with a *full-sized* tiled shower and linen closet; a walk-in closet ideal for skinny non-claustrophobics; and even a laundry room. Our builder was so proud of the laundry room, he actually proposed a glass door for it so that the aesthetic appeal of the new space would not be lost, even to the most casual visitors.

Before any of this could be done, we had to make a serious effort to stabilize the float, which meant properly attaching the bonus log, hitherto attached with little more than one-by-fours and wood screws. It also meant removing 900 pounds of Styrofoam and adding seventeen air barrels. I helped our builder take the Styrofoam to the new dump in Fremont—a monument to dystopia, the living embodiment of *The Waste Land*, a godforsaken place that I hope never to experience again—most likely the final stop for the sofa pieces on their way to oblivion.

Among the next items on the list were: electrical upgrading; a heating, ventilation, and air conditioning system; and real insulation throughout. We splurged on a heated towel rack and bathroom floor. Although most of the jungle scene had to go, we salvaged the painted door that featured the river, some of the forest, and nearly one half of the leopard. Our artist friend came out for a visit, took one look at the sorry remains of the game preserve with the hacked-up big cat, and painted it out in broad strokes of eggshell white.

Our contractor did almost all of this remodel by himself. In his spare time, Ben was also making a fine sangiovese through much experimentation (and fermentation), which may explain why the job took nearly three years. This gave us plenty of time to delve into the mechanics of adopting him, in hopes of getting a friends-and-family rate for his labor.

―――

And here we are today, easily getting in and out on either side of the centrally located bed. We just have to make sure that we never get out on the same side. Or, if we do, that we accept the fact that the place will tilt.

One of the select few members of our community who never had the pleasure of living in our home walked by one day, after all this remodeling was done, when we were once again on tilt, and asked, "Wouldn't it have been simpler to tear the place down, bring in concrete float blocks, and build a brand-new home?"

All I know is, we did our level best.

Stillness
by Lesley Hazleton

I envy cormorants. Watching them from my desk as they hunt for fish, I play a kind of one-sided game with them, trying to predict when they'll dive. I'd do far better playing the lottery.

They're not like cats. There's no staring fixedly at a succulent piece of prey. No tensed, quivering muscles crouched in preparation for the pounce. Cormorants are craftier than that. They feign absolute indifference.

I don't even see them appear. I look up from the keyboard and there one is, settled in the water as though it's always been there and I just never happened to notice before. It's not looking around; in fact, it's not moving at all. I look closely, waiting for a sign. Anything that could tell me it's spotted prey. But no, nothing.

I know that at some point, at some split second, it'll dive, but try as I might, I can never predict exactly when. There's not so much as a twitch, not even the barest swivel of the curved neck or shiver of the feathers. Not the slightest sign. One moment it's there, and then, faster than I can blink, it's gone—an elegant head-first dive, as fluid as the water itself, so quick that I'm never quite sure if I actually saw it or just recreated it in my mind. There's hardly a ripple to indicate where it went under.

I wait, holding my breath as I search the water, trying to predict when and where it'll surface. I never succeed. A radius of forty feet, maybe, and some thirty seconds at a time—that's as close as I get. I focus on one spot, convinced that this time I have it, only for something to register in my peripheral vision and see it already surfaced, a fish in its beak. A quick upward toss of the head and the fish is gone. And then once more, that calm, almost eerily patient stillness, the water in motion beneath and around it, and me at my desk, watching, as still as the bird.

And then comes the dive with no surface that I can see. The cormorant's moved on. The water seems oddly empty, and I feel very alone.

The Big Gray Wolf
It Was Meant to Be
by Ivana Durinovic-Wolf

"You have to let some water drip tonight. It's freezing outside, and your water pipes will burst otherwise," he said. "You don't want that." He shook his head. "Actually, your water should drip not only tonight, but also tomorrow night and for a few more days thereafter. The weather forecast shows temperatures below zero for the next few days."

I was looking at him like he was an alien, somebody not inhabiting this beautiful planet Earth. Who had ever heard of an insane idea like that? Water is the most precious commodity, and it will become even more important in the future.

At that time, I was still a "naive" European, having arrived just shy of a year and a half ago from Munich, Germany, the highest developed country in Europe, a social and economic paradise with the highest planet Earth protective standards.

A few minutes ago, this attractive man had appeared on my doorstep. I first saw his big dark shadow through the tinted window of my entry door. A man in tight jeans and a jean jacket awoke my European old-country memories of old American northwestern movies, a lonely adventurer. His long, curly gray hair framed his smiling face and was pulled into a tight ponytail.

"You must be Ivana, Jerry Callahan's new tenant," he said. "I am Jerry's publisher. She asked me to take care of her house, and"—a long pause—"you, while she is gone."

What a cute charmer. His intentions seemed quite obvious.

But he went on.

"Jerry leaves Seattle each year for her annual trip to Mexico,

Puerto Vallarta, from the beginning of daylight savings time, in November, to the end of daylight savings time, in April."

Jerry was a charming little woman in her seventies who had the most welcoming smile, and was a popular companion of her girlfriends from neighboring docks. Their five p.m. gin-and-tonic gatherings were legendary. I met her in a most unusual way, which later on, I started calling destiny.

Just fourteen days ago I had moved to Seattle and to my dream home, a charming little floating home on the east side of Lake Union: a bohemian houseboat community situated in the center of Seattle, surrounded by the bright lights of Seattle's rapidly growing skyscrapers.

On that particular late morning, I was on Alaska flight 1477 from San Francisco to Seattle. Being a scientist, I was invited to present my work at the highly reputable Benaroya Research Institute, meet with their scientists, and discuss our collaboration. My specialty was medical immunology and genetics. I dedicated my life's work to developing new therapies for the diseases of the immune system. Save humankind, save the world.

Our successful international collaboration had already been going on for a number of years. Within an international project, we were working on developing innovative immune therapies for patients with diseases of the immune system, popularly called autoimmune diseases. The most renowned and common ones were diabetes, multiple sclerosis, rheumatoid arthritis, psoriasis, and many others, altogether more than a hundred described by now, impacting more than 8 percent of the human population. The common denominator of all these diseases was that our immune system, being programed to protect and defend our body's organs from the invading microorganisms, such as viruses or bacteria, by producing antibodies and sensitized lymphocytes, suddenly and mistakenly started attacking and destroying these organs, leading to devastating disease. These diseases were on a frightening exponential rise around the world, particularly in highly developed countries. Seattle was considered a hot spot within the US.

At that time, I was appointed a visiting associate professorship at Stanford Medical School, Department of Immunology and Microbiology, a world-renowned center of this science, but was considering accepting a position in Seattle.

The day was peaceful and sunny, and the flight over northern California wine country, Napa and Sonoma, and the Oregon mountains and coastal areas, was just gorgeous. After opening my laptop and going over my presentation and my notes one last time, I reached for the colorful *Alaska Journal* in the seat pocket in front of me. At first I thought I was dreaming, but that couldn't be true. In the middle of the journal, there were beautiful pictures of charming floating homes resting on the glittering waters of Lake Union in the middle of the city of Seattle. At that moment, I did not have the slightest clue that they existed there, that they existed in the US at all. A complete but extremely pleasant surprise.

My love and admiration for the houseboats, and the bohemian style of life on them, dated from a long, long time ago. At the very beginning of my career, as a young scientist, I was appointed to spend time as a guest scientist in Holland, at the University Hospital of Leiden, the headquarters of the Human Organ Transplantation Center, the Eurotransplant. At that time, it was the booming center of European medical science, the crib of discovery of genetically programmed structures on human cells that regulated immunological reactions, in particular the rejection or acceptance of the transplanted human organ, deciding between life or death of the receiving patient (with a great potential of saving many lives). The head of the department, Prof. Dr. Jon van Rood, was being considered for the Nobel Prize for Physiology or Medicine. Unfortunately, he didn't get it. It went to his three colleagues, one immunologist from France, Jean P. Dausset, one Venezuelan-American immunologist, Baruj Benacerraf, and one American immunologist, George D. Snell.

The tiny country of Holland harbored many kilometers of water canals with picturesque floating homes surrounded by beautiful nature, but also crossed little villages and big towns—cribs of civilization. Local people loved them and incorporated them into their everyday lives in numerous inventive ways; they used them for kayaking, sailing, rowing, and biking, but also skating in the winter when they froze. The unique Elfstedentocht, "Eleven Cities Skating Tour," was organized once a year in the winter when the canals froze and stretched across 135 miles of frozen canals in the Friesland province of Holland.

The most attractive use of canals for me in Holland was living on them—in floating houses, barges, and old ships adopted specifically for that purpose. People, young and old, lived on them in unity with nature, water, wind, animals, birds, plants, marine life, but astonishingly, all that happened in the midst of the most tightly populated part of Holland: in the vicinity of their working places. That was the first time I had witnessed that life. I was watching it from the windows of my friend Diánne's apartment, in the toll shore building where I lived. I was admiring it while biking the canal shores to the lab, from the beach, from the colorful tulip gardens, and from the windows of my lab in the hospital where I worked. I instantly fell in love with this lifestyle. Right then I decided that, sometime in my future life, I wanted to come back and experience it. I wanted to live on a floating home.

Like magic, Seattle had floating homes, and I had just seen them—I was holding their beautiful pictures in my hands. At that point in my life, I was only thinking about moving to Seattle, but at exactly that moment—when I saw the Seattle houseboats—the decision just fell into place. I was moving to Seattle, and I was going to live on a houseboat.

One of the houseboat owners this story in the *Alaska Journal* was dedicated to was Jerry Callahan. My little lady. She was the writer who wrote a fiction book called *Staying Afloat*, the life stories of houseboat owners from the Seattle, Lake Union community: their hopes, desires, loves, joys, setbacks, and destinies. I was deeply touched. There was also a picture of her little old but charming houseboat imbedded in colorful flowers. There was also her e-mail, which I wrote down.

A few months later, as I accepted the position in Seattle, I wrote Jerry a short e-mail introducing myself and asking her if she could help me rent a houseboat in Seattle. The response came instantly, that no, she couldn't help me, but she was leaving Seattle for her regular daylight-savings-time trip in the month of October (the time of my inquiry was the beginning of September), and if I wanted it, she would rent her little house to me until April. She also included in that e-mail a few more cute pictures of her view of the lake from her favorite wicker chaise lounge wisely positioned in front of the living-room window facing the lake. I was ecstatic. Yes, of course I wanted it. This was a great start to my long-desired houseboat life.

I came to Seattle a few weeks before Jerry was leaving to Mexico. The Institute had put me in a hotel nearby to bridge the time before moving into the house. During that time, Jerry was such a gracious host. She organized a party for me on the dock to introduce me to all her charming, friendly houseboaters. She didn't want me to feel alone in a new city. A few days before she left, she asked me to come over because she had to ask a favor of me. Big surprise, the favor was to take care of her little, red sporty car. The parking rule in the neighborhood was that you were not supposed to have your car parked in the same parking spot for more than three days. Every three days you had to move it to the other spot; otherwise, you would be fined by the city officials. With this little, red sporty car coming my way, everything just fell into place. My luck was complete.

Seattle was known for the most pleasant climate in the world. The charming Northwest was famous for perfect moisture and temperatures, nature, islands, mountains, but not at that time of the year. From November to March, it was just wet and gray all the time, skies covered with the drifting ocean clouds drizzling rain. Plants loved it, and the vegetation was beautiful, with blooming camellias and wild cherry trees in January. Temperatures were seldom below zero, and snow was very rare, except on the surrounding mountains, but when the snow occasionally fell, the Northwest world came to a standstill. In the city of Seattle, cars didn't know about winter tires. People just didn't drive, even the busses and public transportation stopped, and offices closed down until the snow melted and life started again. What an interesting world.

Living in Germany, the snow world looked completely different. Cars had powerful winter tires, and people hardly bothered noticing that the snow fell. A part of the nuisance was having to clean your windshield in the morning and plowing the snow on the pavement in front of your home—life was normal.

My big gray wolf never stopped coming back. Now, after fifteen years of an exciting and happy life together, divided between Germany, Croatia, and Seattle, we often fondly think of Jerry and our beginnings in her little-lady flower houseboat floating on the romantic shores of Seattle's east Lake Union. Unfortunately, it didn't survive the fast architectural development of Eastlake. It was recently destroyed and replaced with a beautiful modern structure—the new look of the booming high-tech city of Seattle.

Our houseboat, which my husband passionately describes as one of the oldest and most original—more than one hundred years old—shack. Our shack is a charming place resembling all the history of this Northwest Native American territory, now transformed into one of the fastest growing high-tech regions of the US, the new Northwest American Silicon Valley, the American dream.

Yesterday, we experienced a historic moment, the return of the democratic world in America, a rosy view of the future for our beautiful blue planet Earth.

Love Is a Dinghy
by Florence V. Stephenson

I moved to Seattle in January of 2020 with the hopes that my adventure-soaked single years were coming to an end. The desire for company and affection now outweighed the benefit of starting brunch at eight a.m. without having to wait for someone to get out of the shower.

Two months later, a pandemic would strike out all my dreams of finding love and company.

It took five months for me to get so sick of myself that I started thumbing through dating profiles, looking for someone worth risking death and disease to meet. I rallied my girlfriends for support and took the dive.

———

When you're searching for love in a new city, strange patterns emerge. In Chicago, it was hordes of aspiring comedians. In San Diego, it was men feeding elephants. In Seattle, it was cats.

Cats on your chest. Cats as scarves. Cats in jackets. Cats driving around in Subarus. I captured evidence of at least a hundred cat-wrapped humans, all looking for love in a pandemic. I couldn't see sense in dating someone I was already allergic to, so I immediately cut the cat boys from the dating pool.

I fished through profiles for a week before finding a man who stood out from the rest. He was picture wearing a turtleneck sweater while playing a fiddle on the deck of a sailboat. He had sent a rover to Mars and spent weekends making sourdough bread loaves that would have called me into any bakery had they been set in the window. He shared that his greatest fear was that a playground slide would turn into a giant cheese grater as he went down. I jumped for joy when the Fiddle Man returned my message a few days after I had given up hope. He told me that weekend had been his birthday, and he had gone to Costco to get salmon for his parents. *This was it*, I thought. This man had a Costco membership.

We set a date to meet at Terry Pettus Park. He would come over in his dinghy, and we would have a picnic on the water's edge. I called my friends. They had been rooting for the Fiddle Man since I'd forwarded over his picture, and together we had a good giggle over his dinghy.

~~~

On the walk down to the park, I pulled blackberries off bushes and whistled to the birds, keeping my pace relaxed so I didn't sweat or make myself nervous with excitement. I met a golden puppy named Waffles, who was rolling around in an ivy-covered hill as if it were a bed of fluffy goose down. I ambled my way down the steep Eastlake bank and settled onto one of the splinted bleachers overlooking an Adriatic view of Lake Union.

I wasn't early, but he was late, so I had some time to consider what I would do out there on the lake. How far could I swim if I needed to bail? How likely was it that he was a psychopath?

"I'm here!" I messaged.

"So am I..." he responded. "In a blue shirt and a dinghy."

There was no dinghy here. I pulled up my map and found my location — a pulsing idle blue dot. I leaned in to see the little label that marked my spot at what should be Terry Pettus Park, but which, in fact, was named Lynn Street Mini-Park.

I admitted my mistake to the dinghy boy and counted out all the others that I'd made: was late for the date, went to the wrong place, wore all black on an 85-degree day, couldn't tell the difference between a park and a mini-park, probably forgot to put on deodorant… Five minutes later, I was saved by a small white boat that rounded a row of floating homes. A man in a blue shirt came near, and I stood and waved. He waved back. I continued to stand, looking out at him as he slowly approached, regretting that I had gotten up too soon and not knowing what to do with my hands. I couldn't sit back down, but it was very odd to just stand here staring at him. I took deep breaths and hummed an awkward little tune to myself for a minute and a half as he motored to shore.

He hooked the dinghy up to the dock, wearing a homemade mask patterned with German beer steins and yellow trim. His hair was longer than it had been in his picture, a wild mane of untrimmed curls. His blue shirt was a light linen button-up—a sensible summer choice.

"I thought I was catfished," he said. "There was a woman at Terry Pettus with a black shirt and red bandana, but she didn't look anything like you! She gave me a dirty look when I asked her name."

I apologized, again, as he secured the little plastic boat to the edge of the dock that separated us. He put out bagels and smear, supplied by his sister's bagelry, and I added to the feast with a small wheel of cheese, watermelon, spritzers, nuts, and olives. I dealt with my nerves by spurring him to talk about his work on rovers and asteroids. His enthusiasm for space was what convinced me that he was not a psychopath and that I would very much like him to break social distance by inviting me onto his dinghy. My wish was granted as soon as the bagels were gone. If I knew that was all it would take, I would have eaten faster.

I was out on the lake, touring eclectic floating homes, with a handsome, intelligent, kind man who came with a free bagel source. It was such a contrast from my rainy solitude on the hill these last five months. The Fiddle Man turned around his little boat and brought us home to his bigger boat. A houseboat. A rental because he was a practical romantic like me. We looked out at the city from his balcony and waited for the space station to pass overhead. The stars twinkled their reflection in the water passage below as a neighbor waved at us from a nearby rooftop. We waved back.

The Fiddle Man could have won me over with his sweetness, buying me flowers for my birthday, serenading me with fiddle tunes in the middle of the lake at night, making me sourdough waffles with leftover starter, but it was the houseboat that wooed me home. After only three weeks of dating, my suitor asked me if I would water his tomatoes while he went sailing to Sucia Island. I held out my hand for the keys.

Each day I sat with my feet in the water, taking meetings in that sun as it warmed me from above and reflected up from below. Little fish danced through the milfoil, growing bold as their curiosity to taste my toes grew beyond their fear of me. Pairs of ducks floated past, flaunting their partners and reminding me that I missed mine.

I spent evenings sitting on the roof surrounded by colored Christmas lights that in any other setting would be tacky, but here on the rooftops of houseboats were as romantic as a dinner on the river Seine. Floating homes had never crossed my mind before. I hadn't even seen *Sleepless in Seattle*, but after only a week of being the caretaker of one, I knew that I would not live on land again. Any other life could not be so sweet, I thought, as the gentle rock of waves from a passing boat swept me off to sleep.

My Fiddle Man returned from his sailing trip with a fresh baguette from an island bakery. Between my week on the water and this perfect show of affection, I knew I had found the one. Six years alone, five months of pandemic, one Fiddle Man, a dinghy, and a houseboat was all it took.

Online Dating and an Astrophysicist
by Wanda Wilson

Online dating? What a lame way to find a date or a partner! That was for desperate folks. Nevertheless, that is what I did in the summer of 2015. Without telling anyone, I decided to take a risk by trying out an online dating site for seniors. I was divorced, bored, and somewhat lonely. I thought it would be nice to have a man in my life for occasional company. It was risky for me because I did not want my family and friends to think of me as needing to have a man in my life in order to feel fulfilled, or some such crazy thinking. I had heard the dreadful stories about men meeting women online and then stalking them or cleaning out their bank accounts. Perhaps I was doubting my own self-reliance. Was I that desperate? I had always prided myself on being independent. Heck, I had owned and run a forty-acre commercial orchard for over twenty-five years, graduated from college at age forty-two, and received my master's in education at age forty-five.

But I knew that I could be smart about how I approached this venture because, after all, I was only looking for some occasional company. I set up a new email account that did not include my name. I used a phony name in my dating profile. I decided that I would not give out my phone number or address to any prospective dates until I felt safe. I even considered trying to find a way to set up a profile without using my own picture in case someone I knew recognized me. It did not happen. And thus, I was ready to face the uncertainty and my perceived peril of putting myself out there on a dating site.

I read several profiles on dating sites for seniors. Many were living with their adult children or even roughing it in a camper in the woods. NOT! Then there were those who had precise requirements for the weight and size of any would-be dates, not noticing their own profile pictures displayed double chins and guts hanging out. I had chatted with a few prospective dates but had not had any interest in meeting them. Of course, almost all of them loved candlelight dinners and long walks on the beach. Yeah, right!

However, on a sunny evening in August, I came across a profile photo of an attractive man from Seattle who was obviously out hiking. Hmm. Then I read his profile. I cannot recall precisely what it said, but he mentioned that he was a retired university professor who liked to travel. He was a widower, and his writing passed the scrutiny of this retired English teacher. I figured I could check him out on the University of Washington website since he used his own name—and I did. So, I decided to send him a chat message, and much to my surprise, he responded right away. Unfortunately, at that time he was in New York City getting ready to fly out the next morning for three weeks of work in Europe. He explained that he was an astrophysicist and still working. However, we continued to chat off and on for three weeks. Catching me off guard once, he wanted to Skype then and there, and I freaked out and refused. My hair was a mess; I had no make-up on, and I was wearing sweats. He later told me he was concerned that I had not used a recent picture for the dating site. Still, we continued chatting and got to know one another without all the pressures of looking right or displaying our little idiosyncrasies that might be a turn off on a first date. One of the things we laughed about later was that we were both judgmental about grammar and proper writing styles. I guess we both passed!

After three weeks of sending messages back and forth, we both anxiously looked forward to meeting in person. As fate would have it, Toby was flying into SeaTac from New York about thirty minutes after my flight arrival from visiting my kids in San Francisco. I thought it sounded so romantic, like something out of the movies, to finally meet at the airport. I told my kids about Toby and how eager but nervous I was about our meeting. I tried to not act like a giddy teenager going out on a first date. In my head I was imagining what it would be like: Romantic? Disastrous? Ho-hum? Alas, I got to the San Francisco airport, thinking about Toby flying to meet me, only to be told that there was a four-hour delay in my flight, arriving around 11:00 p.m. Oh, no! The fates were against me.

And thus, our first meeting happened the next day outside a small Indian café close to where I live. I saw him before he saw me. He was wearing a hat, sunglasses, and blue jeans, checking his phone and looking around as though he were lost. I assumed (hoped) that was him, and as I approached, we greeted each other with huge smiles and a handshake. We talked nonstop for three hours about our children and grandchildren, where we had grown up, where we had lived as adults, about our occupations, and so on. We laughed as we shared "outrageous" family secrets, debating who had the best stories to tell. We talked about what we wanted our relationship to look like from that point forward: getting off the dating site and giving this relationship a try. Also, at that meeting I had to explain to him that the name on my dating app profile was not exactly accurate. He thought he had been writing to "Joy Lee" rather than Wanda Wilson. I could tell by the look on his face that I would have to convince him that I am normally not a liar and am trustworthy. I hoped he could understand why I was cautious about keeping my identity private until I felt comfortable. He must have had some faith in me, because we continued seeing each other, enjoying each other's company, acting like young lovers.

He told me early in our relationship that he planned to sell his condo in Fremont and was considering buying a floating home because he was looking for more of a community setting. By then he knew a retirement community was not for him and his active lifestyle. I remember he asked me to come and look at a houseboat his realtor wanted to show him on Lake Union. My thought was, well, okay, but we have only known each other for two months and this is about you. At that time, I had my own place to myself, and I liked it that way. We met the realtor and she kept talking to us like we were a couple. I backed off and reminded her that I was just a new girlfriend, and this was his business. As it turned out, the first listing was just not right for Toby because it was a houseboat rather than a floating home, and it was designed more as a party house rather than a potential home.

I had some familiarity with houseboat living because a few years earlier I had visited a couple who lived on one. I thought these floating homes were very cool with so many odd shapes and sizes and colors. I loved the movement of the home with the wind and wakes. I had never envisioned living in one since (a) I could never afford one, (b) I am basically afraid of the water, and (c) I don't know how to swim.

However, Toby fell in love with and bought the third houseboat/floating home that he saw. He was so excited about it. And I was happy for him. At first, he was not too certain about the bright colors both inside and out; however, he soon realized the colors added to the houseboat community charm. We had a great time (and a lot of hard work) setting up his new home on the water. For me, it was like a vacation house, a wonderful, cozy place to visit since I had my own place. I loved the views from the rooftop. I relaxed with the swaying and movement of the house.

The house started to feel like home for me several months later when it was necessary to remodel the kitchen, and I was an integral part in planning and designing along with the contractor. I got to see my ideas take shape in the finishing touches.

As we continued to spend more and more time together, I

eventually realized we were a "couple." I happily acknowledge that my idea for "occasional" company has become full time commitment. And Toby's cute, colorful, fun house on the water has become home. The "yard work" consists of picking up the occasional plastic or Styrofoam that comes washing up the canal around the house and planting colorful red geraniums in the white flower boxes that accent the porch. The abundant and colorful flowers in the pots along the decks greet me during the summer months. I appreciate the community activities, such as parking-lot clean-up days, potluck dinners—both planned and spontaneous; and an occasional outdoor movie; all of which add contentment and joy to my life on the water with Toby.

By the way, my astrophysicist and I do take long walks on the beach, especially at Cannon Beach, Oregon, and in the winter months we eat our evening meals by candlelight.

A Lovely Life on the Water—or Not
by Spider Kedelsky

Don't believe all the hype you hear about living on a floating home on Seattle's Portage Bay. There's nothing idyllic or romantic about it. It's a living hell. Let's start with otters. Cute, cuddly, fun. So charming to see them frolic in the water. Do not believe it. They are monsters of the not-so-deep. Try cleaning otter crap and regurgitation off your deck every morning. And that damned chirping announcing their presence at any hour.

And pity the floating home owner with otters nesting under her floorboards or a fish rotting on the inaccessible timber beneath the front door, no doubt left by some forgetful, sated furry beast. But try to trap these wily critters and you participate in the ultimate act of futility.

Willing to consume anyone or thing that gets in their way, they are, unfortunately, also very smart, and not one, to my knowledge, has ever been caught by a despairing owner on the edge of otter madness.

Otters not a problem? How about rowers? They make a pretty picture, you say, gliding silently along the water in dawn's early light. Elegant, peaceful, and the very soul of outdoorsy, athletic Seattle. Bosh, I say. Starting at 5:30 a.m. every day, they go flying by our house, oars clattering, rowers grunting, coxes booming, and accompanying coaches in motor boats yelling instructions.

With up to four different clubs and the University of Washington out there on any given morning in singles, doubles, fours, eights, and who knows what other multiples, the water in front of my sweet little floating abode can look at times like Dunkirk redux. Call the clubs and complain, you say? Easier to call the White House and be connected directly to the president.

Rowers not enough? How about boaters? How about lots and lots of boaters? A veritable freeway of them flying by our little dream house on logs in the summer or on a warm, sunny winter day. Christmas boats, Opening Day boats, vacation boats, Fourth of July and New Year's let's-go-see-the-fireworks boats, let's-take-our-boat-to-the-Husky-football-game boats, Sunday driver boats, tour boats, party boats, rented boats, police boats, Emerald City Yacht Club boats, and, God bless them, jet skis. All ply the waters in front of our house. And the sea plane taking off and landing from time to time? Don't ask.

People who visit us often ask, "Does the house move?" Well yes, my dears, it does, when wakes and swells from these nautical nightmares hit it with the force of small tsunamis. We rock; we roll; the logs groan; potted plants topple; the chains holding us in place complain; flotation barrels displaced from under the house pop to the surface like breaching whales; our cats scurry to hide under the bed; grown men cry; and mysterious bangs and clangs heard at no other time emerge from the depths.

Finally, flotsam and jetsam. Know the difference? I do, but who cares? Bottle caps and life preservers, tree branches and two-by-fours, glass containers and displaced paper labels, beer cans and tires, oil slicks and what appear to be vomit slicks, condoms and plastic food bags, logs and ladders, cigarettes and boat bumpers—they all float into the waters around our dock. And billions and billions of little pieces of white and blue plastic foam from broken down or discarded food coolers, coffee cups, insulation, and who knows what else. Recently, even a poor dead beaver.

So this is a horror, no? And I haven't even mentioned the looky-loos coming up our private dock, the milfoil and noxious weeds clogging the waters and grabbing at our legs when we try to swim during the summer, seagulls and crows banging the life out of their catches on our roof, vociferously honking Canada geese and… Well, I could go on.

But if truth be told, there is nothing better than fog over the water in the early morning, the moon reflected off the still waters at night, or Harry the Heron patiently standing on one long, skinny leg, the other tucked up under him, waiting for his next meal to surface.

So I guess you can keep your dirt houses and give me, sigh, my lovely life on the water as I watch the boats and the condoms float by.

Two Midwest Hayseeds Learn About, Live In, and Love a Century-Old Floating Home
by John Macdonald

When we first moved to Seattle, we two Midwest hayseeds never thought about living on a houseboat.

That was certainly the case until our three children had left for college and Sally and I were rattling around in a Richmond Beach suburban rambler. Yard maintenance was now up to us, and the commute to our in-city jobs was getting longer and longer.

And then our sailing friends touted the delight of downsizing to a houseboat with no grass to mow, adding that work would be a walk away.

All that, plus a quiet life on a lake, sounded really nice.

The houseboats we knew of in the Midwest were mostly used as family recreation vessels on the larger man-made lakes and reservoirs. We don't remember ever seeing a floating home being used there as a year-round residence.

In Seattle, once the houseboat bug was in our ear, we began asking around. Our best resources were fellow *Seattle Times* news colleagues, Tom Stockley and Steve Dunphy, already proud owners of Lake Union floating homes.

Tom and his wife, Peggy, delighted in telling us of the goodness of the lifestyle, but weren't shy from noting some possible downsides, such as constant dampness and limited storage, space to entertain, and parking to name just a few.

It was during sailboat vacations to the San Juan and Gulf Islands that helped convince us that life on the water sounded pretty darn good.

A Lake Union floating home seemed just the ticket to that good life.

And so began an adventure that eventually had us falling in love with a century-old floating home.

Our first on-the-water dwelling was a slender two-story model with kitchen, bath, and bedroom on the first floor, living room and two small decks on the second. About 750 square feet.

A narrow staircase went up the east side. When guests of any girth climbed it, the place got tippy and everyone else aboard had to scoot to the other side for balance.

One January night, we went to bed about nine. Outside, big wet snowflakes drifted like gauze through the beam of a streetlight.

About two a.m., it felt like someone was tipping our bed to one side, trying to roll us out. As my feet hit the floor, my mind asked: "How much will we tip before we topple over onto our neighbor's houseboat?"

I threw on some jeans, a sweater, galoshes, hat, and ski jacket, grabbed a snow shovel and scrambled up the ladder to the roof.

What began as a scant evening snowfall had grown to eight heavy inches on the flat roof. And the structure leaned dangerously to the east.

Each shovel-full of wet snow made a loud kersplash as it hit the water below. My footing was slippery, and I was afraid I might become one of the kersplashes below.

Half an hour later I had cleared the east half of the roof, bringing us level again. I crept back down the ladder and into bed and made plans to have a log installed as an outrigger to help keep us level.

That dump of snow didn't faze a seventy-year-old neighbor, however. When she couldn't reach enough of her roof from the dock to remove heavy snow, she tied one end of a rope around her rooftop deck railing and the other end around her waist. Then, snow shovel in hand, she belayed herself down her sloping roof, pushing the snow into the lake as she went.

We watched in amazement and trepidation.

The couple who sold us our first houseboat had moved just down the dock to an older one-story floating home that had an old-fashioned bowed roof. A year or so later they retired to the San Juan islands. We bought that houseboat from them, too, and followed them down the dock.

Our education about houseboats continued.

An annoying knocking sound came from under our living room floor. We doubted it was an animal, but perhaps? We worried that a major floor support had failed.

We feared major repairs.

"Not necessarily," a neighbor said. "Call Art Holder. He can help."

Art, we quickly learned, was one of the indispensable and genuine characters in the Seattle houseboat community. He was a wiry middle-aged guy whose ruddy complexion announced more than just a few days in the sun. He has an extensive education, we were told, but we never figured out why he chose shoring up floating-home foundations as a career.

When Art arrived, he headed to our deck and disappeared under the house between the flooring and the slimy log raft that keeps us afloat. Minutes later, he crawled out, brushed off some algae that clung to his shorts and shirt, set his Indiana Jones hat at a jaunty angle, and strode off down the dock looking ready for a fancy dinner.

The knocking under the floor was no more.

We learned a lot from Art that first summer about our "new" floating home. For one thing, he pointed out, it is one of the early floating homes on the lake.

Stories abound from a century or more ago about fishermen, loggers, and dock workers who lashed stray logs together as rafts and scrounged what wood they could find to add makeshift walls and a roof. Anything that could be had for very little money to keep the rain and cold out.

Later, as the rafts grew into homes, forty-five-foot-long old-growth logs, some as big around as a whiskey barrel, formed the foundations. If they're kept submerged, they last many decades. Ours are originals, Art said.

Stringers—hefty six-by-eight-inch treated beams—are placed across the logs to provide the base for flooring. Art said our stringers were soaked and soft and coming apart. They needed to be replaced if they were going to keep the houseboat up out of the lake.

I learned even more watching Art work. First, he spent a lot of time just staring at the logs.

"Thinking," he said with a scowl. I learned pretty quickly not to interrupt him when he was thinking.

As the days went by, Art began to open up, though grudgingly, about what he was doing. He had to float in the new stringers, lift the house off the old ones so he could get them out of there, and slide the new ones in place. And he'd do it all by himself.

I pestered him with more questions, including why he had to do so much thinking.

"Fussing with those big, heavy stringers has to be done in just the right sequence," he muttered, especially since he was doing it alone. If he missed a step, a stringer might pop loose and cause major damage to the houseboat. If his timing was off and he lifted the houseboat too much, it could cause the walls to twist and come apart.

Using a crude barge as a staging platform, Art poked and slid a long canvas-covered hose—the kind firemen use—atop the logs beside an old stringer. When he pumped water in to fill the hose, it lifted the house just enough so he could pull the old stringer out and slide the new one in.

A few days later, I learned first-hand what Art meant when he told me how the walls might twist.

I had come home early to change clothes to play tennis. Art was at one corner of the houseboat using a jack placed on a log to lift the houseboat just a bit higher than the hose would do to clear the way for a new stringer.

Inside, I could hear creaks and groans as if the whole houseboat was wrestling the jack. And, in front of me, a bedroom wall was separating from a window casing. Just a bit, at first. Then more. Now an inch, then two. I could see daylight between the wall and the window casing.

Was the whole house coming apart?

I rushed outside. "Art," I hollered, "should we be concerned that the wall and the window casing are separating?"

Art looked up with a patronizing grin, followed by a scowl at being questioned.

"Be happy that's what it's doing." He grunted. "When this jack is down, those walls will come together and be as tight as ever."

He was right. A dab of paint covered the once-separated seam. And it has never leaked a drop.

Every new houseboat owner wonders how old the place is. Many still contain some evidence of their early years.

When Art pulled the flooring from our small east-end room, he found that someone had cut about ten-foot lengths out of two side-by-side end logs. Through the void, I could see the lake.

"The toilet and kitchen sink were probably right here when this room was built," Art said with a smile. "The waste just went into the lake."

Today, we're on the city sewage system.

In a later remodel, we moved a wall to make room for a washer/dryer unit and found another surprise, one that gave us a more precise date for our houseboat.

Those early houseboat builders often used old newspapers as cheap wall insulation.

But our wall yielded something special—a faded yellow cardboard-like "mat" used in the newspaper printing process. The soft pliable sheets were perforated with letters and set into a cylinder-shape mold into which lead was poured. When the lead cooled and hardened, it was put on a press to print the newspaper.

This mat was in perfect shape, clearly showing a full page of the *Seattle Star* for Friday, December 26, 1919. More than a century old, and you can read every word.

Art taught me the history of our bowed roof, too. It is arched, with the middle a foot or so higher than the sides.

Those early builders used boards about six inches wide and an inch thick to support the roof. They soaked the boards until they could be bent from wall to wall across a ceiling joist and nailed into place.

"Cheap, easy, and amazingly strong," Art said.

Right again.

One summer we invited friends over for a rooftop cocktail party. About thirty came. Being a worrier, I scrambled around the place throughout the party, looking for cracks or hints that the roof might collapse under all the weight. It didn't.

A few years later, after a heavy snow, a friend calculated that our bowed roof was supporting more than 4,000 pounds of the white stuff. We've not worried since.

Our floating home has coughed up other surprises for us, too.

Ben Ridgway, a one-man construction crew we hired for a decade-long, off-and-on remodel, chuckled when he showed us what he found when he removed some of the interior walls in the living room.

Wooden two-by-fours, which were supposed to be installed vertically floor-to-ceiling and spaced a foot or so apart, served as studs to support the walls and ceiling. But a number of our studs weren't supporting anything. Every third or fourth two-by-four nailed to the floor didn't reach the ceiling. And several of the boards that were attached to the ceiling didn't extend all the way to the floor.

"Amazing that the walls just didn't collapse," Ben snickered.

A few days later, he shook his head, smiled broadly, and pointed to a large wooden ceiling joist that stretched most of the length of the houseboat.

"What about it?" I asked.

"See those black areas, kinda like charcoal?" he said. "Signs of electrical fires. Lucky this place didn't burn all the way down."

There aren't a lot of children on houseboat docks. Too dangerous, some parents think.

We found out why, first hand.

A few months after we moved into our century-old new abode, we had a family dinner with swimming and boat rides for entertainment. As her brother and parents walked down the dock to go home, Ashley Wallace, our nine-year-old granddaughter, as kids that age will do, skipped and danced her way down without a care.

But she came too close to the edge of the dock. Kersplash, right between the houseboat and the dock. Thankfully, she bobbed straight up and Colleen Temple, her aunt, grabbed her by her hair and blouse collar. Had she gone under the houseboat logs or under the dock, she might not have come up at all.

The next week, we had a shelf built to cover the open space. Today, it supports flower boxes and keeps folks from falling in.

One of our neighbors, a safety-conscious dad, had another idea to make the dock safe for his daughter. He nailed two-by-fours along the edge of the dock all the way from his house to the shore to keep her trike from rolling into the water.

Seattle's houseboats have gained worldwide attention, much of it because of the 1993 movie *Sleepless in Seattle*. It starred Tom Hanks, Meg Ryan, and a floating home on the west side of the lake.

Rarely does a summer week go by without tourists from all over the globe wandering, all bug-eyed, down our dock, cameras clicking, fingers pointing, and tongues wagging in many languages.

There's always someone in the group who speaks English and can translate our answers to their questions.

Tourists always ask to see the *Sleepless in Seattle* houseboat. So we march them to the end of our dock and point across the lake to the houseboat in question. Cameras click and click and click and click, even though it's a quarter mile away.

And then they turn to more personal questions about houseboats: "Do you get seasick?" "Isn't it awfully damp?" "What about water creatures? Do they come into your house?"

A German TV crew once used our deck as a staging area to film a documentary about our houseboat community. We've seen the film, but our German isn't good enough to know what they said about us.

~~~

During the Goodwill Games here in 1990, Russia sent its education minister as a representative. As a reporter, Sally was allowed to join his group on a tour of the city.

While they were chatting, the minister said he had heard about Seattle's floating homes as ways to escape busy city life. When she told him she lived on one, he got excited. "Could I see it?"

As the Soviet entourage strolled down our dock, the Russian talked about his large and fancy dacha on the Black Sea. At the time, our houseboat was undergoing one of those major remodel projects. He looked around at the eclectic floating homes up and down the dock then back at our home-in-progress. He paused, and pointing to the rubble in the water and close-by neighbors, said, quite sincerely, in a heavy accent, "Yes, but why would you want to live like this?"

Sally explained, but he wasn't convinced.

When Midwest friends visit, their lips often say, "What a delightful way to live."

But thinking of the small living space and lack of a yard, their eyes sometimes say, like the Russian, "Why would you want to live like this?"

As the two of us age, we sometimes ask ourselves if we want to move to more comfortable environs. Perhaps a larger place with a bigger bathroom.

We think about it. But where else could we find such a fascinating bunch of neighbors?

Like the neighbor across our dock who had a six-by-eight-foot wooden raft outfitted with an old shrimp trap for a table, plastic chairs at each corner, and an electric motor to propel it around the lake. On calm summer evenings, she and her friends would don fancy hats like those of bygone days and cruise the lake. While having snacks and wine, they greet curious passing boaters with raised wine goblets and ask, snootily, "Might you have any Grey Poupon?"

Or the other neighbor who cut a foot-square hole in his living room floor so he could fish from his easy chair. Sometimes he drops a couple bottles of wine down into the lake to cool.

As new, bigger, fancier floating homes are built and floated into nearby slips—some even have basements!—our century-old, one-story, bowed-roof buddy does look out of date.

Sure, we could tear it down and build a new one. One with a big second story and a rooftop deck with a three-hundred-sixty-degree view of the lake, the city, and the Olympic Mountain Range.

But as we nudge into our eighties, perhaps we're a little out of date ourselves. Our thirty-year love affair with this old floating home is still alive.

As we say:

The place is old. And so are we.
And that's okay. We think we'll stay.

SPECIAL COCKTAILS—Four former DOX residents; from left, Shirley Lashua, Darlene Madenwald, Kit Woods, and Bev Matson enjoy afternoon libations on Darlene's raft, *Bon Ponton*.

Our 100-plus-year-old houseboat

Thea Yeannakis, left, introduces her pet duck, Jelly, to toddler, June Villanueva, during a DOX gathering.

Plunge
by Susan Jostrom

Early in the morning, for 365 days straight, we peeled the feather comforter off the bed, placed our naked feet on the floor, tugged on a swimsuit, marched the ten steps to the water's edge, and leapt in. Four years ago, my husband, Mike, and I agreed to swim every day for a year. Living on a houseboat on Lake Union means the water is lapping, literally, at your doorstep. "Swim" is slightly inaccurate, as really the goal was simply to leap in and climb out like child's play. This act felt nothing short of heroic for a couple of reasons. One, we were the only people on our dock at the time who even jumped in the water in summer or winter, and two, although Seattle has a rather temperate climate and the temperature of Lake Union reaches seventy-three or four in summer, it hovers around forty through the lingering winter months. Frost and snow are not common in Seattle, but not rare.

We agreed to jump into the lake every day, even through the long drizzly winter because, we both concur, swimming in cold water is good for you. Benefits of cold-water immersion include lower immune system response, better sleep, lymphatic drainage, improved circulation, improved metabolism, mental strength, more energy and—look it up—increased libido. The list goes on. None of these reasons, however, are why I jumped in every day for a year. I am a little reckless, a little uncontrolled, and a little spontaneous. But that's not the reason I jumped in. I leapt into cold water every day for a year because it was exhilarating. Euphoric. Fun! I continue to this day, although not daily, and have yet to regret a cold-water plunge, even on those miserably foggy, frosty mornings in winter.

Regardless of those frosty mornings, the main rule of our "swim" was to go all the way under water. A dip to the shoulders did not count. As with many things in life that challenge us, it is the anticipation—the anxiety, fear, worry—of requisite action that defeats us before we even begin: it's too hard, too long, too cold, you're too busy, too tired, too old. It was, therefore, easiest to get the plunge over with as early as possible every morning so the event did not hang over us the entire day like a lurking vulture. If we were feeling timid, we climbed down the ladder. If the ladder was the choice du jour, the rule was you had to let go of the ladder and actually tread water or even swim a few strokes. On extremely brave mornings in winter, we would paddle about for four or five or even ten minutes, every breath a short, swift cloud. On occasion, a meandering goose or a diving cormorant in full majesty of their winter plumage would float by and eye our naked skin with shame as if to say, "*Where* are your feathers?" Or a neighbor would glance out the window and shake his or her head, no doubt muttering, "*Fools!*" No joke, it was very hard to stay in that forty-degree water. But it was over soon enough, and by 7:30 a.m. or 8 a.m., after a hot shower and a cup of black, steamy Starbucks, we already felt like conquerors, as if by this one brief act we could sweep the stars and moon from the sky and command the sun to rise.

The following year we modified the goal, and instead of a daily plunge, we agreed to swim in salt water at least once a month. This was hardly a challenge, as we took several trips to tropical waters that winter. Except in January. In January, we reminded each other daily that we needed to drive out to Golden Gardens and take a plunge in the fifty-degree salt waters of Puget Sound. Daily, we agreed we would do it. Tomorrow. Sure enough, January 31 was upon us and we had no choice but to climb into the car with swimsuits on under a layer of winter clothing and head for the beach. It had to be one of the coldest and windiest days of the new year, a classic winter day in Seattle with low coal-colored clouds hovering and gray rain sleeting sideways. Golden Gardens is an idyllic sandy beach and picnic area normally swarming with families in the summer, barbecues lit, and the aroma of grilled hot dogs swirling in the air. This day, there were a handful of hardy, red-faced souls strolling the beach, bundled in foul weather gear, hands deep in their pockets, braced against the wind-whipped shore. As I said, it is the anxiety of requisite action that too often defeats us. The drive from our floating home to Golden Gardens is about twenty minutes with no traffic, and believe me, my heart was pounding. That nemesis anxiety was getting the best of me, and I seriously questioned the validity of this nonsensical goal. And then we arrived. With my metaphorical horse blinders strapped on, I had the door open before we were fully parked, slipping off my pink Crocs, dropping my fleece-lined pants, tugging my purple Smartwool zip-up over my head, strapping my Crocs back on, and racing through the rain toward the unfriendly and frigid salt water. There was no dabbling of toes or swishing of water around my middle, with gleeful hands in an attempt to get used to it. It was an all-or-nothing go-for-it, like a berserker roaring into battle. I leapt in shoulder-deep then dunked. Gasping, wiping salt water from my eyes, my skin bristling with fire from the cold, I raised my hands in victory. WHOOOOOHOO! The foul-weather-wrapped sturdy Seattleites walking the shore hardly even looked our way, as if to say, "I've seen that before."

Seattleites are not milksops. You bet it rains here. A lot. If you want to plan an outdoor event around the weather and you don't want to get wet, you may as well stay inside and read a book. On any given day in summer or winter, you will find hordes of weather-resilient bike riders, walkers, runners, sailors, kayakers, and rowers. And a few people who plunge into the cold water of Puget Sound in winter.

I am not a newbie to cold-water plunging in winter; rather, a lifetime of leaping and swimming and more than once soaring off our twenty-one-foot-high houseboat, of cajoling others to jump with me (*on the count of three, go!*). Once, in the small hours of the night after sharing more than one bottle of Our Daily Red, I said to my across-the-channel neighbors Tim and Tania (names changed to protect the innocent), who were over for dinner, "How about a swim?" Within minutes, no, seconds, they were stripping off clothes and jumping from the first-story deck. We laughed and splashed and hollered before they swam home. In the morning I gathered shoes and clothing and paddled their belongings across the short channel. There is little more bonding among new friends than vaulting unclothed into the dark night and deep water. This conniving has worked well with other new neighbors, but I will refrain from naming more names and telling more tales of late-night houseboat-leaping cajolery.

We have passed on this cold-water vaulting to our children. Once, a few years back, my son tried persuading a group of buddies to jump into Puget Sound with him while attending a weekend wedding event in Poulsbo. Mike and I had sailed over in our Hallberg-Rassy for the wedding and were overnighting in the marina. Peter and said buddies came sauntering down the dock toward our boat on the afternoon of the wedding. "Mom," he said, "wanna go for a swim?" Without hesitation, I shrugged and said, "Sure!" I casually garbed myself in my swimsuit, dropped the swim ladder, and dove in. Apparently, Peter had been trying to persuade them to go for a swim with no success. Knowing what he knew, he said, "If my mom goes in, will you?" "Haha, sure," was the mutual response. I looked back at the boatload of buddies, their mouths agape. One by one, as if in slow motion, they banished their nerves, pulled their shirts off, and jumped in. While sailing home from that same wedding event, we witnessed a group of about five swimmers, men and women, no one wearing a wetsuit and accompanied by a chase boat, swimming across Puget Sound from Bremerton to Alki Beach—a distance of about ten and a half miles. Later that same fall, we watched another group of men and women swim from Alki Beach out and around a point of land and disappear. We watched for ten or fifteen minutes, and they did not reappear. Again, they were clad only in swimsuits, swimcaps, and swim goggles. This seems superhuman to me, but a good example of how we can push our bodies past preconceived limits.

This past New Year's Day, we took our annual polar plunge in the icy Whitefish River in front of our tiny 1918 cabin in Whitefish, Montana. My friend Karin joined Mike, me, our son Peter, and his girlfriend, Sarah, along with a small group of enthusiastic invitees as we slid and shuffled through the half-foot of snow and ice toward the river's edge. One plunger was eight-year-old Finn, who clearly won the prize if there was a prize to give, as he was in and out not once, not twice, but three times, even obeying the "all-the-way-under" rule. I grinned when my youngest son, Gabe, later sent a photo of himself clothed in his swimsuit, hair dripping, proudly standing at the shore of a beach on Long Island Sound. One neighbor I was certain would take the plunge, did not. As we later stood around the campfire, sipping hot cocoa and musing over the great way to start the New Year, especially washing away 2020, the neighbor commented, "I just couldn't figure out a reason *why*." "It's good for you!" I responded and continued my rant on deaf ears.

Yes, you can die in cold water. Yes, many people die every year in cold water. But case studies indicate most do not die from hypothermia, rather from cold water shock and the gasping reflex, which can involuntarily cause you to swallow water if you go under. "Jumping into very cold water causes a whole host of responses," says John Castellani, Ph.D., research physiologist at the U.S. Army Research Institute of Environmental Medicine. "As soon as you hit [the water], receptors in your skin fire up your body's cold-shock mechanism: you lose control of your breathing and end up gasping and hyperventilating. Your heart starts racing, your blood pressure goes up, and your stress hormones soar. It can take about two minutes to get control over everything again. Research shows that after about five sessions of being purposely exposed to really cold water (about fifty-three degrees) for just five minutes, that cold shock response diminishes by more than 50 percent." In other words, you can adapt. I have witnessed men and women *swimming* for hours in cold water. Like Reinhold Messner climbing Mt. Everest without supplemental oxygen, like world-record holding free-diver Herbert Nitsch, who has reached a depth of 830 feet and can hold his breath for over nine minutes, we can train ourselves to reach beyond what seems humanly possible. Nitsch says, "Each time I think I've reached a limit, there is a door…it opens… and the limit is gone."

Wim Hof is another good example of pushing limits. He is known as The Iceman and has immersed himself in *ice water* for up to two hours. He planned a seminar in Seattle the spring of 2020, which, imagine that, I signed up for. Suggested preparation for the day-long seminar included cold showers for up to five minutes. It was not mandatory to participate in the ice baths at the seminar but highly encouraged. The event was unfortunately canceled due to COVID-19 *(oh, sweet relief!)*. I cannot lie; my fear and anxiety were high over the anticipation of sitting in ice water with strangers, trying to prevent my teeth from chattering and my lips turning blue.

It bears repeating: the anxiety of an event that is difficult—the fear, the worry—whether it takes two seconds or two weeks or two years to complete, is what often defeats us before we even begin. You know the FDR quote, "The only thing to fear is fear itself." You are the only one who can defeat you. We need to take risks to learn anything in life. If you want to learn to swim, you need to get wet.

My Ironman neighbor, Eagle, can be seen almost daily (donning a wetsuit in winter) plunging in and swimming laps along the frontage of the Eastlake houseboat community. Although I crave the water and love to swim, I am not this dedicated. (*Too hard! Too old!*) My friends, Bob and Dianne, college swimmers now in their early sixties, still drive an hour one way, three times a week, to work out in a pool. I am not this dedicated. *(Too tired! Too busy!)* But there is nothing more soothing or meditative than an occasional slow, smooth crawl stroke across the lake when breath is deep and controlled, the water caressing like silk, and my mind is released from the rumblings of the world. I am free.

I have not yet jumped in the water today, and it is 6 p.m. in January and very dark and very foreboding, and I am very cozy and warm by the dancing flames of the fireplace in our living room and have no desire whatsoever to leap into the unwelcoming water. *(Too late! Too cold!)* I am sipping a glass of Cabernet, purchased from our own personal wine cellar, Pete's Grocery, just a skip and a jump down the street. Three deep-green Glassybaby candles flicker on my concrete coffee table while a pot of pinto beans and red peppers simmers on the gas stove. A sliver of moon is watching me through my living room wall of windows, wondering, *Will she, or won't she?* Lights from Queen Anne hill reflect across the water in streaks of gold and silver like stalagmites rising from the depths to meet the shore. The Space Needle stands guard over the unruffled water. Like a dream, like a dare, the water waits outside my door.

The author plunges into the Whitefish River in Montana

It Takes a Floating Village
by Andrea Adams

One late afternoon in August of 2018, a sense of welcome surrounded us as my husband, John, our real estate agent, and I found our footing along a gently bobbing, squeaky dock of quirky floating homes on Seattle's Lake Union. The golden glow of late afternoon sun reminded us of a favorite Zulu word, *ukushona kwelanga*, which translates into "the time of day when everyone looks beautiful." This community felt so cozy—although we had not been looking at houseboats to buy, we stopped by this one out of curiosity. This was supposed to be a lark—getting a feel for a different lifestyle. John and I were considering selling our family home, but was it serendipity that we found ourselves looking at a floating one?

As empty nesters, it was time to lighten up and have fun. We were looking for a fresh start. Our family home held tension from memories with our son, Peter—we had struggled to help him as he battled and raged with lifelong mental health problems.

We wondered if houseboat living might give us the pleasure of water sports, the arts, and local restaurants. There would be fewer cycles of home repair and extensive landscape projects.

We traveled down the walkway of a dozen floating homes, our eyes dancing over yellow, blue, green, and red cheerful houses perched on flotation. Flowering pots of red geraniums greeted us, surrounded by cascading tiers of pink begonia, sage lambs' ear, and orange nasturtiums in hanging baskets. Artisan frogs, a mosaic table, and wind chimes added whimsy. Kayaks and sailboats bounced lightly in the waterway alleys between the homes.

It was new, yet familiar to me. Years ago, when I lived in a duplex across the street from this very floating home dock, I made a friend, Laurie, who lived on a floating home two docks over. She and I started a book group that still continues. I'd also attended many fabulous Fourth of July parties on her roof, where the professional fireworks display never failed to evoke wows. If we bought this floating home, Laurie and I would be just two docks apart. Our *still thriving* 1986 vintage book group could have double the fun on Lake Union.

As we arrived at the slip, John and I walked over a little gangplank and up a few stairs into a compact, barn-red, two-story home that was the second-to-last dwelling on the lakeside dock. Inside, the wide-board wooden floors had an appealing, imperfect look because they'd been repurposed from a previous life in a warehouse. The original owner had thought of everything to make it functional, comfortable, and filled with the presence of sky and water. From the southern windows, we could get a glimpse of the Space Needle and the full Seattle skyline.

The upstairs was complete with a built-in, all-glass reading nook that faced out towards the lake so we could see boats, bridges, and seaplanes—a veritable children's book illustration in live action. I felt a fresh breeze from the lakeside French doors, which quickened my pulse. We could breathe here. Even in the winter, I imagined that it would feel good to be in this house looking out at the rain.

A driftwood gray table invited me onto the deck. The rocking of the dock, the meditative lapping of waves against old wood, it all lulled me into a dream state. Paddleboarders drifted by, one with her wagging dog sniffing the breeze as if to scout out what changed from yesterday. We could see Lake Union all the way to the Fremont Bridge facing west. Sunset views would be spectacular.

Back inside, with the scent of beeswax, the soft sound of our steps on those wide, planked wooden floors, the tidy, intimate feel of the place, it all gave me a feeling of being at home. I could see that John, too, was delighted. Was it the houseboat's warm glow of cherry trim, the built-in desk areas for each of us, or maybe the manageable scale of two bedrooms downstairs?

We climbed up the spiral staircase to the roof, thinking about how this floating home was designed to make the most of the slip in which it was docked. It had been pulled by a tugboat all the way from British Columbia, Canada. Twinkling lights were in the buildings on the horizon, the peach glow of transition to evening on the ripples of the lake. Holding hands, we looked out in each direction, whispering about an imagined future of gin and tonics with scintillating conversation right where we were—in fact, we pictured making no changes to the furniture on the magical rooftop deck.

"Uh oh," we said, exchanging smiles of unexpected certainty that we must buy this new home.

Living on the lake would be different from living on rural Bainbridge Island. We would be in the middle of the city yet peacefully surrounded by water, with an abundance of waterfowl for my birder husband to identify. Our kayaks and paddleboards could just tip off the dock into the water whenever we liked. The whole scene felt vibrant. Would the community be as connected as I imagined?

The closing was in September, and we moved in October, a quieter, less social time of the year than summer. As we unpacked, we noticed the hanging flower pots had been taken down, and the roof-deck furniture was tied to rails so it wouldn't bang around in windstorms. All the Dutch doors were closed so we wouldn't hear our talented neighbor playing Mozart on her piano or notice the scent of pancakes and bacon as we had when we were buying the house in late summer.

Our immediate neighbors welcomed us with wine, and after determining a bit about us, including our politics and our appreciation of a white Bordeaux, hinted that we might want to join their annual month in Italy the following year. Another neighbor brought her famous chocolate chip cookies. Across the way we saw the eclectic art collection and handmade harpsichord of another set of neighbors. Tantalized, we knew it would be during the good weather that we'd really get to know everyone.

Christmas came with the opportunity to host the annual party for my long-time book group. Along with laughing, drinking wine, reading *A Child's Christmas in Wales* aloud as we always did, and eating dense, dark gingerbread with fresh whipped cream, we reminisced about our first meeting at Laurie's.

"Can you believe we were only in our twenties and early thirties?"

"How many of us were single then?" I asked, laughing.

"Oh, yeah, we know a few . . . *interesting* historic details," said Laurie, raising an eyebrow and winking.

As John and I settled in and began our relaxed new life, our troubled twenty-one-year-old son, Peter, also seemed to be finally on a more even keel. Were the episodes of bipolar swings leading to arrests, violence, and self-harm behind us? We hoped so. I have a wonderful Saint Patrick's Day memory of him visiting us on the floating home when we were listening to jolly tunes of Irish music. He took this silly, little green hat off of our small dog Darla's head and placed it on his big head. He seemed to relish the time together as much as the corned beef and cabbage. Our daughter, Natalie, and granddaughter, Kenzie, were staying with us for the weekend and joined in the celebration. Peter left with an extra heaping container of corned beef, roasted carrots, potatoes, and many slices of Irish soda bread for the next day. Peter did love to eat, and he was fun to feed, a big, strong, handsome young man, who worked out for hours a day and had the appetite of a lumberjack. We were inordinately happy when he was able to enjoy our get-togethers.

In April, we'd helped Peter move from the YMCA "Young Adults in Transition" program into his own place in West Seattle. I'd signed up for dog training classes near his apartment to have a casual reason to stop by, take him to lunch, and see how he was doing without overtly hovering. He had a job and seemed smitten with a new girlfriend.

Then, in May, John and I got the devastating news that Peter had committed suicide. We'd moved heaven and earth to try and save him. In the end, we couldn't.

Lake Union was a refuge for me as I worked through my grief. Sometimes I looked out over the water and was momentarily buoyed by the colorful sailboats, industrious groups of rowers and gorgeous merganser ducks gliding by with their ducklings. One tough day, overwhelmed with grief, I wound up on my friend Laurie's gently rocking floating home roof, having a glass of wine with book-group friends. This gentle support and somehow, even a bit of laughter, helped me to cope and carry on.

However, the generosity of this new community went even further as we began to plan our son's memorial service. Even though our floating home community was new to us, to our stunned gratitude, four households of very new acquaintances offered their homes for our guests to stay in during the June weekend when we planned to have our memorial service. We knew it would make a big difference in our ability to casually gather with our out-of-town guests. We had lots of good friends on Bainbridge Island, where we lived for twenty-five years, but *giving up their houses for our guests*—it wouldn't have occurred to anyone—not just in our town but I'd say that would be true for most places in the USA. There was an unusual openness, a generosity of heart and spirit in the floating home community—an extraordinary kindness.

The beloved book group pitched in by getting photos developed and setting up a gallery wall of our son. They went to Costco for me, made marinade for the chicken, and helped me and my brother, who'd flown out from NYC, prepare Asian noodle salad and grilled chicken for the arrival dinner for everyone who came from out of town.

The memorial-service weekend arrived. Right next door, in a modern, artistic floating home, my stepfather, a brilliant San Francisco liberal, shared the space with Scott, a New Mexico conservative on whose ranch Peter once worked and went to school. Scott had a few free hours, so he climbed in his rental truck, turned on country music, and went to visit another boy who had been on his ranch. He got stuck in the middle of Seattle's gay pride parade, dividing around his truck like a river around a rock.

"I never seen anything like this crazy town," he told us.

My stepfather, Bob, slapped his knee and smiled at Scott. Polar opposites. Earlier that day, Scott had mentioned that he didn't believe in climate change.

My stepfather, who had conducted international forums on a sustainable planet, didn't know what to make of a man, living so close to nature, who didn't recognize the urgency of the climate crisis.

"Here is a diagram of what it takes to have a sustainable 2050," he said, showing Scott a detailed, extensively researched visual explanation that took a year of collaboration.

"God won't let that happen," Scott replied.

Yet they extended mutual respect and genuine curiosity as they shared meals and conversation at our floating home. We'd all been part of "Team Peter," helping him make it through his childhood to the best of our abilities.

The service was held at Plymouth Congregational Church.

The most moving words the minister said that day were, "He knew that he was loved."

Since Peter so loved food, our last song (his favorite) was sung right before the reception. "Food Glorious Food" from *Oliver*. We were touched that several young people said that our Peter had saved their lives. Our son had taken what he learned from years of therapy, found his voice, and given comfort to others who struggled as he did.

The morning after Peter's service, yet another dock couple, he, a yoga teacher and physician, and she, an expert on etiquette, provided much appreciated quiche, fruit, and pastries from their favorite bakery for all our guests. All we had to do was to keep the coffee pot full and the stories flowing. We felt incredible gratitude for my stalwart book group and this generous and increasingly dear houseboat community—their tender, buoyant embrace.

Getting to Tui Tui
A History Illustrated in Stamps
Story by Janet Yoder
Stamps by Robby Rudine

VISITING A HOUSEBOAT

1973. My boyfriend, Robby Rudine, and I were living together in Olympia while attending the Evergreen State College. One evening, we went with a friend up to Seattle, specifically to Portage Bay, to visit a friend of his. We sat in the living room of her houseboat and watched the lights of the University District reflect across the surface of Portage Bay. We listened to the water lap against the log float and felt the houseboat gently shift. Her home was cozy. This gracious woman put on a pot of spaghetti sauce, another pot of pasta, and made a simple salad. We ate. We visited. We fell in love with her houseboat.

GETTING ON THE LAKE

1974. A wild, crook-tailed, big-eared kitten named Doodley Squat got us onto the lake. We found her flying around a wine supply shop, bouncing off bags of sugar, off shelves, off carboys. The store owners said they were going to take her to the pound at the end of the day if we didn't take her home. We took her home in a paper bag that looked and sounded like the Pow! Pow! Pow! of Jiffy Pop at peak popping. Only problem: Our apartment did not allow pets!

I tried to keep this hyperactive kitten from destroying our apartment while scouring the classifieds in search of a place where we could have a cat. On a whim and a memory of magic, I looked under *Houseboats*. None were for rent, but one was for sale, and the owner was having an open house that day.

I made my way onto a narrow dock on the north end of Lake Union's east shore to find two single-story houseboats. The sprung-roofed, inside moorage one was for sale. I walked into this charming, funky houseboat. In the living room was a three-foot-tall, built-in, foam-padded, bigger-than-a-bed platform in the corner with forest-green carpet running from the floor up and over it. The carpeted platform with throw pillows along the walls formed a gathering space where we could sit cross-legged against the wall and stare out the window to the north at the small live-aboard fishing boats and across the water to Ivar's Salmon House.

The price was $8,000. The moorage fee was $50 per month. We had jobs, so we pulled it together and moved ourselves and Doodley Squat onto the houseboat. And then we met Garney.

GARNEY

Garney Harris (our lakelord) was born in, owned, and lived in the house on pilings at the head of the dock and owned the dock (all one property) where we moored. When we met him, he was old, grumpy, and modified every noun with *god-damn*: god-damn hippies, god-damn developers, god-damn city, god-damn green flies swarming around god-damn dog shit in his yard—oh, and the god-damn houseboats. Okay, we knew he wasn't our new best friend, and we knew our houseboat had to have moorage, so we addressed him as Mr. Harris, paid our moorage on time, and tried to mostly stay below his radar.

Garney didn't like it when we invited people over, didn't like interacting with people, didn't like people coming down his rickety dock to the two houseboats, and didn't want us to complain about the rotted planks in the dock. When we did complain, he rolled some tarpaper along the whole length of the dock so we could no longer see which boards were rotted and which were missing altogether. I remember the feel of nothing but tarpaper under my foot. We learned where not to step.

One weekend, Garney was staying down the street at the home of his gal friend. So, we went to Ernst Hardware at University Village and bought some lumber to replace the rotted planks. We knew we didn't have permission, so we worked fast to roll up the tarpaper, crowbar up the old boards, then cut and nail down new ones. We worked our way down the dock, then rolled the tarpaper back over our work. The supports below were still rickety, but the wood we stepped on was solid. Tarpaper was no longer our structural support.

Garney made a point of telling me that no feminine products—"Women's things, you know"—could go into the toilet. When any of my three sisters came to visit, he would remind me to tell them too. He had a point in making this request. At Garney's we had a moorage that included a sewer line that ran to a tank with a pump that—unless it clogged—pushed everything up to the sewer pipe under Fairview Avenue. Without such a moorage with its legally required sewer line, our houseboat could have been hauled off and sold for scrap or burned for fire-fighting practice by the Seattle fire boat crew.

Nevertheless, nothing can compare to that first summer on the houseboat. In the evening, we sat on the deck to watch the northwest sky turn magenta and gold before it darkened into night. Friends found us. They came over to swim, to share a potluck meal, to sit on the deck or the living room platform we now called the green hump because of the way it humped up from the floor in all its green-carpet splendor.

FIRST WINTER

Then winter arrived. We discovered the houseboat leaked air from around every window, through cracks in the walls, even up through cracks in the floor. It turned out the houseboat was built on three different cedar log floats lashed together. When the houseboat moved, the floats pulled apart and then pushed together, bumping into each other like big sluggish disco dancers. This created openings for cold air. We hung rubbery weatherproof curtains on the window along the green hump. We wore REI layers of long underwear, sweaters, down vests, thick socks, and knit hats.

There was a cranky oil furnace that had two settings: hot as Hades or off. We were afraid the houseboat would burn down if we left it on at night. So we started each morning in the chilling cold. One morning the water in the toilet had frozen solid. Winter also brought rain leaking through the skylight in the bathroom, where we discovered mushrooms growing out of the rotting particle-board flooring. The beams below the floor joists of the houseboat were rotting as well. No wonder the former owner sold this houseboat at the height of summer. We made it work that winter and waited for the return of days of warm sunlight reflecting off the water and shimmery evenings sliding into night.

ATTRACTIVE NUISANCE

When we first moved onto the old houseboat, our next-door neighbors were older fishermen who lived on their fishing boats on the dock to the north of us. We always waved and said hello, but I have no idea what they thought of us: hippies hosting parties and jumping into the lake with a lot of whooping. Now the historic motor yacht Linmar moors at that same dock and gets rented out on weekends via Airbnb. Mostly it doesn't bother us unless guests are there for a loud party. Time cranks around.

So many friends and family came and stayed that we applied the term "attractive nuisance" to the houseboat. The term implies the houseboat presented a danger and we were inducing others to endanger themselves by coming over. And if they were hurt by this danger, we were at fault because we presented the attractive nuisance. The real danger was that they would fall in love with the houseboat and want to stay forever. Or at least for the summer.

ANOTHER WINTER

Another winter blew in and the cracks in the walls and floors grew larger and leakier. We caulked. But the three log rafts torqued the houseboat whenever the wind blew or a police boat raced by, as if an evil chiropractor were cracking the place apart. Robby and I hit our own coming apart. He returned to Texas to work for a film and video production company, and I went to Mexico to study Spanish and teach English. Friends moved onto the houseboat.

We returned to the houseboat a couple of years later and found it had deteriorated more. We had to do something. We asked a friend to draw plans for a remodel. All we had to do was get Garney's approval.

THE BATTLE OF GARN

We invited Garney over to show him the plans and a small model of what we proposed. He bent to look at the model, then straightened back up, turned red in the face, and shouted, "No! No!! No!!!" He marched out of the houseboat and up the dock, steaming and sputtering. The next day, he left a handwritten note in our mailbox that said, "There shall be no exterior remolding."

We saved the note because we loved the word *remolding*. It so well described the condition of our houseboat.

Things escalated. We thought we should have been able to remodel because the houseboat was unlivable. Garney thought we should not. He increased our monthly moorage rate, more at one time than he was legally allowed to do. We fought the increase. Discussions ended in shouting matches. Around this time, I took a teaching job down in Portland. Robby stayed in Seattle but not on the houseboat. By 1980, no one lived on the houseboat. It had become derelict.

After lots of back and forth, Garney sent us and the other houseboat owner an eviction notice. But we could not up and move a floating home. There was no place for either houseboat to go. We couldn't vacate. So Garney filed an unlawful detainer action to get the houseboats off his property. A court date was set.

1982. Our best bet to fight the action was a recent Seattle law called the Equity Ordinance, which was meant to help houseboat owners avoid losing their houseboats—their equity—by providing strict controls on evictions. The law looked good on paper, but there was no guarantee it would hold up in court. Garney was asserting his right to evict both houseboats and change the use of the property. His right (and the right of other dock owners) to do this had not been tested in court. We were the test.

Robby got his friend Dan Rader to represent him. He also called on the advice of Terry Pettus and Bill Keasler of the Floating Homes Association. This organization helps floating home owners fight evictions or acquire their moorages by establishing a co-op or condominium for a whole dock. They wrote the Equity Ordinance we were relying on. But having no precedents for that law was making everyone nervous for our case and future houseboat evictions.

The night before the trial, Robby and Dan were antsy, so Dan's wife, Marla, cast the I Ching, a traditional Chinese means of divination achieved through the tossing of coins. The idea was to settle our nerves by seeking guidance from this ancient source of wisdom. The result was the fifty-eighth hexagram of the I Ching, with Tui above and Tui below, thus Tui Tui. Tui signifies the lake, which we took as a good sign. The I Ching told us that "perseverance is favorable."

So, Robby and Dan did their best to persevere in court. But the judge made an initial ruling in favor of Garney, a ruling that indicated he might declare the Equity Ordinance unconstitutional. A jury was chosen. It was getting serious.

During a break, Dan asked Robby, "What do you think Garney really wants?"

Robby said, "He wants to live in his house and not have to deal with the dock, the houseboats, or us."

Dan took that in. Then he said, "What if you made Garney an offer to buy the property at a below-market price while granting Garney life tenancy in his house?"

So, an idea was scratched out in the hall outside the courtroom. Amelia Schultz, who owned the other houseboat—and whose one-hundredth birthday we celebrated in 2015 aboard the Virginia V steamship—agreed to put in money in exchange for a long-term lease. A deal was made, and the houseboats were saved. Also, the idea of Tui Tui was born. Oh, and the name of the judge was Liem Tuai (pronounced Tui).

On September 23, 1982, money and a property title changed hands. We refer to it as the Treaty of Garn. Garney bought a new car and continued his level of vodka consumption, as measured by the empties that rattled around in the back of his new car. He was still grumpy, but he was no longer the owner of the dock nor the ruler of our destiny.

DESIGNING TUI TUI

After the trial and the Treaty of Garn, Robby and I were saving our relationship, just as we were saving our little place on the lake. Robby came down to visit me in Portland. We sat at my kitchen table and talked through our ideas for the houseboat. A fresh start. Our own design. Robby drew the first plan on graph paper at that table.

We designed the houseboat around the I Ching. The built-in hot tub at its center has eight sides, each side representing one of the eight trigrams of the I Ching. Together the eight trigrams make up a Bagua—a feng shui energy map—that charts the sequence of the trigrams, which relate to each other through astrology, astronomy, geography, and geomancy. The Tui trigram points toward the west door, toward the open water of Lake Union. The design would leave clues so that if the houseboat was ever found adrift, future archeologists could reconstruct our cultural references and be able to moor it in the right direction, to take advantage of the solar design and Tui alignment.

We drew it up and submitted plans to the city. The City of Seattle likely did not get that many applications to build new houseboats in 1983. They erred on the side of caution. They asked for the Shoreline Application, the structural plans for the float, specifications on the support beams, and data on the greenhouse. We brought them everything: calculations for R-value, specifications for the water-source heat pump, the solar panels, the float sump pump with its required alarm.

Time went by with no response from the City. One day we just went there. We found our plan reviewer and asked about our permit. He unrolled our plans on a tall table and we gathered around. He looked at us and back down at the plans. Then he picked up a pen and signed the approval right in front of us. We were ecstatic.

SO WE BUILT IT

1984. The new float was all one piece! Two Fremont Tugboats, *Standfast* and *Barf*, towed the float from Roanoke Reef to our dock while Robby and his crew pounded floor joists onto the moving float. After nothing happening for years, everything was happening at once. We moored up to our pilings now in the outside position, got an electrical drop, and gathered tools. No need for a level or a plumb bob. As our crew was building, I was driving a GMC pickup truck all over town to get beams, joists, lumber, WonderBoard, nails, screws, tile, grout, pipes, faucets, valves, drill bits, and drawer pulls—plus lunch for everyone.

It took a year and a half to build the houseboat, with a break for our wedding on May 18, 1985, on the unfinished houseboat. On December 16, 1985, we moved onto the houseboat and claimed Tui Tui an independent nation.

TUI TUI: ACCOUTERMENT AND DIPLOMACY

The narrative of a tiny nation born of an I Ching coin toss continues over time. We determined our ancient trade coinage—the Tuit. A friend sewed the Tui Tui flag. Another friend carved the Tui Tui coat of arms. (Robby painted a tile of the coat of arms for Lynn Street Park across from Pete's Grocery.) Robby documented Tui Tui's history through stamps (see page 157). He made stamps of the Tui Tui trade coins, the flag, and the coat of arms. He made stamps of us as benevolent rulers, of Amelia Schultz as neighbor extraordinaire, of attorney friend Dan (Attorney Admiral of Tui Tui), of Marla who cast the I Ching, and of the Floating Homes Association for its silver jubilee. To this day, we print visas to issue to those crossing our border. We explain the history to visitors using these Tui Tui artifacts and encourage them to find the Tui hexagrams built into the houseboat.

Thinking of your home as free and independent helps you consider what impact you want your nation to have on the world around it. As Tui Tui citizens, we became involved in creating Fairview Park with its P-Patch, dock, and stairway up to Eastlake. As Tui Tui citizens, we find ways to support the Floating Homes Association, Eastlake Community Council, the Center for Wooden Boats, and the Pocock Rowing Foundation. Much as nations practice diplomacy, we find common ground, or common water, with our neighbors. Over time, we even developed neighborly relations with Garney and complained together about the god-damn developers. When Garney's lease on life expired, Robby commemorated his passing in stamps.

TUI TUI IN THE WORLD

It turns out people are attracted to the idea of a floating independent nation. Argosy Tour boats added a spiel about Tui Tui. If the windows are open, we can hear the guide say. "Tui Tui is an independent country. They issue their own stamps, and they don't pay taxes." We always fear the tourists will be a group of IRS auditors who will go back to their office and launch an audit of Tui Tui. Ride the Ducks put us on their tour for a while. We would hear, "Halloooooooo, Tui Tui! Looking good," followed by a cacophony of kazoo quacks. The stately steamship Virginia V gives a short toot of its unmistakable steam whistle when passing by. If we are in the mood, we step out to wave the Tui Tui flag at these vessels of visitors.

A German film crew doing a piece on Seattle houseboats came to document Tui Tui. Then HGTV came calling and Tui Tui was on *Home, Strange Home*. It was fun. But recently a friend forwarded a YouTube video he came across of a trendy young couple who travels all over the world and posts videos to prove it. Unbeknownst to us, they arrived at Tui Tui, climbed on our west deck, and peered in our windows, shooting video. They could see Tui Tui was under repairs (because rot never rests), could see we weren't living there, and they shared that information with their 22,000 followers. That is where the attractive nuisance could get dangerous!

Despite that invasion of privacy, we do want to introduce others to Tui Tui. We have agreed to be on the Floating Homes Tour whenever they will have us. It is one way of paying back the organization that helped us during our eviction trial and continues to help the quirky community of floating homes.

Tui Tui is our fishbowl, a place where those boating or paddling by can get a glimpse of our particular—perhaps peculiar—houseboat nation. Really, all houseboaters live in the fishbowl. It's what we have bought into. But we keep swimming around, living our stories, sometimes sharing those stories with others, much as the lovely woman on her Portage Bay houseboat once did with us. Sharing the magic keeps it alive.

Art

With wildlife and water right outside their doors, these artists captured their peace through varying expressions. Though the city may be near, they slowed down to depict moments in time spent with the colors found along the dock, ensuring history is preserved.

Cheryl Carlson

150 ~ Landless in Seattle

Jack Quick

"...to sail forbidden seas." —Melville A/P-2

Jackie Helfgott

This sketch was done with the Urban Sketchers Seattle in June 2016 at the Fishermen's Terminal with the original post that went with the sketch on the Urban Sketcher Seattle website. I finally bought a houseboat in 2019 and forgot I had written this!

Today was a special sketch outing at the original site of the 1st Seattle Urban Sketcher's outing seven years ago. Happy anniversary, sketchers! I zoned in on this boat because I have been fantasizing for some time about living on a houseboat. I think this one officially classifies as a boat, but it has that houseboat aesthetic and everything I think about when I dream of my someday floating home. While I was sketching, a little duck swam under my feet, and I didn't even notice until after I took her picture that she had a couple of little babies following. The person who lives on this boat...a long-haired guy who I would have loved to talk to but was too far away...threw open the back door, and I was happy to see it was purple inside, which inspired me to make the water purple.

Robby Rudine

1987 Tui Tui stamp for the Silver Jubilee of the Floating Homes Association

Tui Tui Stamp Day 2005, includes Tui Tui Coat of Arms

Souvenir sheet for the 100th birthday of Amelia Schultz, issued aboard the Virginia V, June 20, 2015

Stamp depicting Tui Tui's ancient trade coinage—the Tuit

North Fairview Courier Route

The Co-Tyees Dragonfly and Dogfish in full regalia on Tui Tui definitive stamps

Landless in Seattle

Abolition of the Plumb Bob for Tui Tui houseboat construction

"Get your ducks in a row" North Fairview Courier rate memorial stamp for Garney Harris

The Co-Tyees of Isle Regis, a semi-autonomous floating island of the Archipelago of Tui Tui

Tui Tui Stamp Day Issue for 2003

Landless in Seattle

Partial sheet of Tui Tui stamps to honor the Floating Homes Association's show on houseboats at the Museum of History and Industry in 2013

The mailbox made by Co-Tyee Dogfish was exhibited in the show called *Still Afloat: The Contemporary History of Seattle's Floating Homes*

Tui Tui first stamps issue of March 16, 1984 (nine months before Independence)

Tui Tui flag stamp: the canton is the semaphore Yankee (carrying mail, dragging anchor)

The field shows a hexagram "Tui"

Attorney-Admiral Daniel Luke Rader, whose inspired treaty making saved the Equity Ordinance that protects Seattle floating homes from loss of moorage

Marla Beth Elliott, who cast the fateful I Ching that gave Tui Tui its name

Tui Tui's Little Free Library Rate stamp, designed by the late Brad Burns and letterpress printed by Day Moon Press

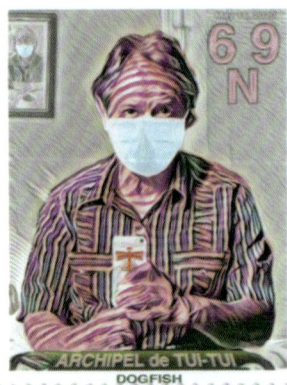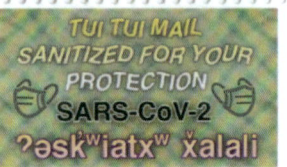

70th birthday stamp for Robby Rudine

70th birthday stamp for Janet Yoder

Lon-Marie Walton

Houseboat Dreams

Sara Zin

Landless in Seattle ~ 175

Don Bell

BLUEBERRY GALETTE
Makes: 2

Ingredients: ½ cup butter, 1 ¼ cup flour, ¼ tsp salt, 1 tsp sugar, 2-3 tbsp ice cold water, 1 cup blueberries, ¼ tsp cornstarch, 1 tsp lemon juice, pinch of sea salt, ½ tbsp sugar, 1 egg white

Directions:
1. Cut the butter into slices and freeze for 3 minutes.
2. Combine the flour, salt and sugar in a large bowl.
3. Remove the butter and using your fingers, combine the butter and flour mixture into large crumbles.
4. Add the ice cold water 1 tbsp at a time. It should not be sticky, so you may not need to use all the water.
5. Roll into a ball and wrap in plastic.
6. Refrigerate for 1-2 hours.
7. Split the dough in half and roll out into a thin disc about 1/8 inch thick.
8. Wrap in plastic and refrigerate for 1 hour.
9. Preheat the oven to 375 degrees F.
10. Wash the blueberries and dry them.
11. In a bowl combine the blueberries, cornstarch, lemon juice, sea salt and sugar.
12. Pour the blueberry mixture into the center of the dough and fold in the edges. Make sure to squeeze the edges closed, so it doesn't unravel during baking.
13. Crack 1 egg, keeping the egg white and whisk.
14. Using a pastry brush, coat the top of the dough with the egg white, then sprinkle sugar on top.
15. Bake for 35-40 minutes, or until the top is golden.

In memory of Don Bell: engineer, architect, boat builder, husband, father, Darcy's friend, news junkie, Doxster, Renaissance man, and all-around great guy.

Poetry

Often a misunderstood artform, poetry comes directly from the heart but is shared with exquisite care. With thoughtfully chosen words, these poets will leave you pondering deeply about homes with water beneath their floors.

My Home
by Karen Lorene-Bell

Fifteen years roll by
As my body grows old and out
Filo dough skin, ribbed raisin bunions
Age sits light as sunshine
heavy as harsh rain
Fifteen years in this coffee line
waiting and sharing a neighborhood
waiting for a barista to
create my cup of coffee

Music thrums and thumps
We are a small, masked crowd
Coffee ready, I give a smile of thank you
"See you tomorrow," understood

I head down toward the water
Accept this moment
Silent
wishing I had called to the young behind me waiting,
"Dance!"
Yes, you, Dance
Yes, me Dance!

We live on water
silent as waves lapping
warmed
by who we are
by a moment shared
houseboat neighbors
coffee
enough
an uphill walk
enough
a moment captured

Living, for Now, on Lake Union
by John Nelson

Beneath my floor: twenty feet of fishes.

And beneath them: rusting, rotting wrecks:
centuries of sunken logs, misplaced flowerpots,
lost screwdrivers, glasses, wallets, keys,
abandoned toilets, burned-out barbecues,
misadventured boats and unwise cats;

Dead things, those, though not forever:
slow or fast, they go to life again,
each in its own way...

Above my floor: more water,
collated by bark or pelt or skin
(—dry boundaries,
thin pretense of separation from the Lake—)
some of it self-conscious,
some of it imagining itself more obdurate
than the junk below.

Live things, we, in this water house, though not forever:
slow or fast, the patient, patient Lake
wins us back again.

Photography

Through a lens, these floating homes residents have stopped time so everyone can appreciate seasons spent off-land. Their days are suspended in time, and these photos are windows into their experiences.

Mikelle Ackerley

Believe it or not, this photo was taken on a chilly and beyond beautiful December 2020 evening on South Lake Union. Winter paddleboarding is a surprisingly popular activity among locals, usually paired with a wet suit or big parka.

Where else in the world can you jump into your back yard? A very whimsical visual of a common activity around Eastlake's floating homes. This photo here is a new resident taking a morning swim after a training run.

Ardis Burr

Queen Ardesia being carried to the water at Canal Boatyard, November 2011.

Awaiting Queen Ardesia to arrive at my home in Eastlake, February 2018. I built my little house for me and my cat. Now it's home to me, my husband, and my dog.

Jackie Helfgott

This photo was taken January 15, 2020 just over a month after I bought my houseboat. I had just run around Lake Union and the snow had started to come down hard. When I walked through the marina gate, I caught this sight of the row of houseboats amidst the snow.

This photo was also taken January 15, 2020 when I rounded the corner as I walked onto the marina dock to go to my houseboat. It was the most magical moment to walk onto the snow-covered marina. In the winter the marina is the most peaceful place on earth.

This photo shows the quietness of the evenings on the Marina in the winter. It is remarkable how insulated the marina is in the middle of a major metropolitan area in the city of Seattle. Walking onto the marina is like walking through the Narnia wardrobe.

This photo was taken on November 6, 2019 while I was getting the inspection done on my houseboat. When I decided to take the plunge to buy the boat, I had no idea my first adventure would be to ride it to the Canal Shipyard to get the inspection and to power wash the hull. That's me in the window. I was in there with my amazing realtor Danny Varona who saw a friend of his as we were floating by so he asked him to take this photo. It's hard to describe the thrill of riding your house down the lake to the shipyard.

This is my houseboat getting power washed at the Canal Shipyard. When the tug boat got us there, I was asked to jump off my boat while it got washed. It was a blast to watch and it was well worth the ride across the lake. I can't wait until the next time.

I took this photo as I came into the marina after running around the lake. I had seen the rainbow while running the Lake Union trail and raced in to catch the sight of it behind the houseboats.

Kevin Humphreys

Lake Union winter sunset

Shaya Lyon

The sound of a heron taking flight over Lake Union is an unmistakable, undignified, single squawk. A visiting heron, however, is quite the opposite. This heron, which spent an entire evening on the roof of a floating home at the 2019 Fairview dock, didn't make a sound.

A hummingbird rests in a tree on a Log Foundation dock at 2019 Fairview Avenue East.

Snow falls on the Log Foundation docks at 2017 and 2019 Fairview Avenue East, in Eastlake. Queen Anne is visible across the lake.

Snow-covered logs in the channel between Wandesforde Dock and the dock at 2201 Fairview, in Eastlake, looking out towards Queen Anne.

A dusting of snow on the 2019 Fairview dock brings unparalleled magic.

Residents of the 2019 Fairview dock replace the chains that hold the floating homes in place. Each fall, residents of the dock gather for a "winterizing party." The neighbors walk the dock together and check each home's water, gas, and sewage hookups, as well as their chains, ahead of the winter storms that could jostle and dislodge these critical connections. Chains do rust over time, and occasionally they need replacing—a logistical challenge that sometimes requires more than one pair of hands.

Log Foundation member Stan Lorenson takes a break during a dock winterizing party at 2019 Fairview.

Gene Morris

Landless in Seattle

Landless in Seattle 215

Adam Nathan

A live bird losing a staring contest with a bird statue

Summertime at DOX, one of the first floating home cooperatives in Seattle

A giant, inflatable Holstein cow sent by Dairy Farmers of Washington to celebrate National Dairy Month

Watching the Fourth of July fireworks up close from Eastlake

The old dock at the Roanoke Reef Marina, empty on the eve of replacement

Towing our under-construction floating home to a temporary barge in order to install a staircase

Looking out at Mallard Cove through a new window

Roanoke Reef on a sunny day

Samantha Skal

The Seattle skyline on a cold but delightful February morning.

Lauren Wilcox

Moorage space is precious, and our 1955 Chris Craft is an extension of the home and a cherished piece of history.

Trading the quintessential backyard BBQ for a family float. When the sun is shining, we're in the "back yard."

Summer dinners are exceptionally special when you live on the water. Time slows down, and you quickly forget you're at the edge of a bustling city.

There's nowhere to hide when you live in a floating home surrounded so closely by neighbors, boaters, and rowers. The pros easily outweigh the cons, and it's relatively impossible to be upset about the views you may have otherwise missed.

After the storm

There's something refreshing about splintering wood and creating a place to gather. Especially in Seattle, the sound of a crackling fire and steady rain on the roof—it's somewhat of a PNW soundtrack.

Closing Thoughts
by Danielle Harvey

Thank you for reading, viewing, and enjoying this anthology. With so much ahead, this was an opportunity to experience the past and present of floating homes history. These stories and pictures reflect the colors of Seattle, Washington, where so many creative people call home. This anthology took work, much beyond my own efforts, and seeing it come together has been a privilege.

When you have a moment, walk down to the water and appreciate the peace it gives so many of us. Whether you're a floating homes resident or not, joy and water are intertwined.

I hope this is a book you'll pick up again and again to constantly live your version of life on the water.

Thank you, L.W. Egret, for the reflections of a landless life captured in these photos that pulled this collection together.

Thank you, Amalia Walton, for your valuable input that led to a cohesive, aesthetically pleasing book, with the contribution of your photos and sharp eye for detail.

A special thanks to Heidi Dellafera Eagleton, for without her, this would have remained an idea. Her push to bring everyone together, with all forms of art, is the reason our readers get to hold this book in their hands.